IN TEN THOUSAND PLACES

In Ten Thousand Places
Dogma in a Pluralistic Church

By
PAUL G. CROWLEY

A Crossroad Herder Book
The Crossroad Publishing Company
New York

For my mother

on her eightieth birthday

1997
The Crossroad Publishing Company
370 Lexington Avenue, New York, NY 10017

Printed in the United States of America

Library of Congress Cataloging-in-Publication Data

Crowley, Paul G.
    In ten thousand places : dogma in a pluralistic church/ Paul G.
Crowley.
        p.   cm.
    "A Crossroad Herder book."
    Includes bibliographical references and index.
    ISBN 0-8245-1698-2 (pbk.)
    1. Dogma.   2. Religious pluralism—Catholic Church.   3. Catholic
Church—Doctrines.   I. Title.
BT22.C76   1997
230'.01—dc21   97-20777
                                                                    CIP

Contents

Acknowledgments

I wish to thank Santa Clara University for supporting research for this book with research grants from the Terry Foundation and the Franzia Family Endowment, and with a sabbatical leave during the 1996–97 academic year. Several people at Santa Clara University deserve special thanks: Denise Carmody, chair of the Religious Studies Department, for reading an early draft and offering valuable practical advice and encouragement; Jim Reites, S.J., my former department chair, who was generous in granting me the leeway to work on writing projects; and President Paul Locatelli, S.J., for his support of Jesuit scholarship at Santa Clara. The late John Carmody, Senior Research Fellow, who introduced me to Rahner's thought when I was an undergraduate at Stanford, read an early outline of this book, and inspired me to write. Nor should I forget to thank the students who, over the years, have taken my "Tradition and Interpretation" seminar, in which many of these ideas were discussed. Not least, I wish to thank my rectors, John Privett, S.J., Gerald McKevitt, S.J., and the entire Santa Clara Jesuit Community for strong fraternal support and encouragement over many years.

I also owe a debt of gratitude to the Jesuit Institute at Boston College for a generous fellowship that provided the time needed to complete this book and to work on other projects within the stimulating environment of the Institute. The following people at Boston College deserve special thanks: Joe Appleyard, S.J., rector of the Jesuit Community, for the generosity of that community's hospitality; my research assistant Ted Kepes; and Susan Humphrey and Joe Curran at the Jesuit Institute. I also extend warm thanks to all the Jesuits of Roberts House, who offered the gift of companionship during my sabbatical year. In particular, I wish to express my deep gratitude to Michael J. Buckley, S.J., Canisius Professor of Theology and Director of the Jesuit Institute at Boston College. At one time my doctoral adviser and now a brother Jesuit, he has offered unstinting support and encouragement through the years, not only to me but also to numerous others, at the Jesuit School of Theology at Berkeley, at Notre Dame, and now at Boston College. I am honored to call him both colleague and friend.

Some of the ideas presented here appeared in embryonic form in my dissertation completed at the Graduate Theological Union at Berkeley. At this time I would like to extend a belated thanks to David Stagaman, S.J., and John H. Wright, S.J., of the Jesuit School of Theology at Berkeley, the justice John T. Noonan, Jr., formerly of the Boalt Law School at the University of California at Berkeley, and Dr. Ted Peters, of the Pacific Lutheran Theological Seminary in Berkeley. I would also like to acknowledge Dr. Ileana Marcoulesco, who introduced me to the work of Gadamer at Union Theological Seminary in New York many years ago. My later participation in her International Circle for Research in Philosophy at the Menil Foundation in Houston provided the impetus for this book. Creighton University and University of Pennsylvania allowed me to present some of these ideas in the form of invited papers at conferences on the thought of John Henry Newman.

I also wish to thank James LeGrys of The Crossroad Publishing Company in New York, who waited patiently and offered much helpful advice.

This book is dedicated to my mother, Doris Crowley, who together with my father, the late Charles A. Crowley, taught me by example the truth of the "dogma" that God works for the good in all things (Romans 8:28).

PAUL G. CROWLEY, S.J.
Santa Clara University
Santa Clara, California

Preface

For Christ plays in ten thousand places,
Lovely in limbs, and lovely in eyes not his
To the Father through the features of men's faces.
                              —Gerard Manley Hopkins[1]

W hen Hopkins wrote his poem, he could not have foreseen
     what the Church of Rome would become in a hundred years'
time. The "world church" so aptly described by Karl Rahner[2] is now
a rich pageant of experiences, theologies, and readings of the tradition of faith. More than any other communion, the Catholic
Church is an archipelago of cultures, languages, traditions, experiences, and theological perspectives—each part finding symbolic
unity in Peter but, in actual fact, irreducibly distinctive. One would
have to go back to the first centuries of the church, even before the
great ecumenical councils, to find such a richly variegated texture
of faith throughout the Catholic world. The course of conversation

---

[1] From "As kingfishers catch fire," in *Poems,* 4th ed. rev. (Oxford:
Oxford University Press, 1970), 90.

[2] See Karl Rahner, "Basic Theological Interpretation of the Second Vatican Council," in *Concern for the Church,* vol. 20 of *Theological Investigations*
(New York: Crossroad, 1986), 77–89. In this essay Rahner demarcates
three epochs in the history of the church: the early church of Palestine; the
church of the Hellenistic world, later becoming the church of European
culture and civilization; and, in our own time, the church of the whole
world, tied to no overarching culture or civilization.

in today's church often looks more like the map of the tangled Los Angeles freeway system than the linear Via Appia leading straight to and from Rome. When the International Theological Commission addressed this situation in 1990, it described "a worldwide crisis of tradition" threatening the very unity of the church. The Commission called attention to the need not only of mediating the past to the present but also of "mediating between different cultural traditions." There exists a need not only for a vertical mediation of the tradition into the present moment through authoritative teaching in dogmatic propositions, but also for concurrent horizontal mediations between and among specific inculturations of the tradition within the communion of faith called the church. This latter type of mediation is a more complicated process that takes place at the levels where faith is transmitted among actual persons living in specific times and places throughout the world.[3]

As recent history demonstrates, even authoritative church teaching, which might aim to bring certain questions to a definitive conclusion, often fails to do so, and can even itself become a source of disagreement within the church.[4] While the normative teaching voice of the faith tradition within the Catholic Church remains the hierarchical magisterium, it is becoming increasingly apparent that merely invoking that authority does not automatically guarantee concord among the multitude of interpretive viewpoints within the church that express variant theological opinions.[5] Contemporary

---

[3] International Theological Commission, "On the Interpretation of Dogmas," *Origins* 20/1 (May 17, 1990): 1–14 at 3.

[4] John Mahoney notes that a major ecclesial development in the wake of *Humanae vitae* was the wide range of responses to it from episcopal conferences around the world: "In the more than thirty episcopal statements which resulted . . . we thus have a body of widely-based literature which views *Humanae vitae* from the standpoint of local churches and is also in a position to comment on the widespread critical reactions to the encyclical." *The Making of Moral Theology: A Study of the Roman Catholic Tradition* (Oxford: Clarendon, 1987), 272.

[5] This was especially evident in the reaction to the "Reply to the *dubium* concerning the Teaching Contained in the Apostolic Letter *Ordinatio Sacerdotalis*," issued by the Congregation for the Doctrine of the Faith on October 28, 1995, in which the teaching of *Ordinatio Sacerdotalis* was said to belong to the deposit of faith and "has been set forth infallibly by the ordinary and universal Magisterium. . . ." See *Origins* 25/24 (November

moral questions, issues of liberation theology, and intramural topics such as the ordination of women raise dogma itself as an issue.

The question I raise here is how dogma can function as an instrument of unity within a pluralistic ecclesial situation, one in which a variety of perspectives not only complement but often contradict one another over the proper interpretation of the content of faith. This book, then, is about dogma and its function as an instrument of unity in the church. The problem dogma faces calls for a reappraisal of the function of dogma within the current ecclesial situation. The aim of this work is therefore modest: to inquire whether we can retrieve a sense of dogma in which it can be seen as an instrument of unity because it is an instrument of mediation of the faith tradition with the people of God who live in widely divergent cultural universes. The need is urgent for such a retrieval of the unifying function of dogma when the means for attaining the unity of the church has been raised as an open appeal in papal teaching itself.[6] It is my hope that this book will further contribute to the discussion.

Whenever the topic of unity is raised, the ecumenical dimensions cannot lie far from view. While the present discussion concerns the unity of the Roman Catholic Church, and most of the references are to issues peculiar to that communion of faith, I hope that some of this discussion will redound to the reflection necessary for the greater ecumenical project, the communion in faith and service of all Christians in what has sometimes been called the "Great Church."

While I will address the meaning of the term "dogma" at length in chapter 1, it is important to understand at the outset that it is intended here, in a broad (and ancient) sense, to include not only authoritative church teaching but also the modes whereby the church's faith is confessed, particularly in and through liturgy. In his important but little known work *Dogma unter dem Wort Gottes*, Walter Kasper stresses that dogma has not only a "missionary-kerygmatic"

30, 1995): 401–5. While this reply does not (and could not legitimately) hold that the teaching itself is infallible, it does judge it to have been given within the ambit of the church's infallibility.

[6] *Ut Unum Sint*, Encyclical of Pope John Paul II, May 30, 1995. See *Origins* 25/4 (June 8, 1995): 35–58.

function—that is, a teaching function for the church both *ad intra* and *ad extra*—but also a "liturgical-doxological" function—that is, that it emerges from and addresses the church's life of faith.[7] Both functions see dogma not as a fortress of propositions to which the faithful must submit but rather as a sign of the gospel within the living faith of the church.

Ordinarily, dogma is thought to suggest church teaching alone, and this is indeed its primary modern sense. As I use the term here, it includes not only extraordinary exercises of the magisterium (dogmas formally defined by councils or popes) but also various ordinary teachings, especially those that are the object of ongoing interpretation within the church (e.g., disciplinary directives regarding ordination that emanate from Rome). I include, then, not only those "dogmatic" expressions of faith that are clearly *de fide divina* (e.g., the Incarnation and Resurrection of Jesus Christ, and their articulation in the Nicene Creed or the Chalcedonian Definition), and those that are *de fide divina et catholica* (e.g., the canons on grace of the Council of Trent and those of the First Vatican Council on faith and reason), but also those dogmatic teachings that are either proposed as *fidei proximum* (authentically taught doctrines such as the moral teaching of the church) or which are proposed as an authentic and intrinsic part of the faith tradition that is confessed and taught, without which the inner core of the tradition would not cohere (e.g., the apostolic succession of the episcopal office).

However, I also intend another, less formal, sense of dogma as the mediation of the confession of faith that has taken place through the great monuments of the tradition. Here the emphasis lies not so much on what dogma says as on how it functions within the life of faith. Dogma as a function of the confession of faith, as confessional theme, would therefore include liturgical traditions (e.g., infant baptism), universal disciplinary practices (e.g., priestly celibacy), and even theological traditions (e.g., Chalcedonian Christology) that have not only served the cause of authentic catholic unity in the church but have also become points of controversy in various times and places. This book, then, wishes to keep alive a broad sense of dogma, one that includes both its teaching and confessional dimensions.

---

[7] Walter Kasper, *Dogma unter dem Wort Gottes* (Mainz: Matthias-Grünewald, 1965), 134–35, 137–38.

Dogma has been the subject matter of several works by Catholic theologians in recent years. Some of these have dealt with the problems and inadequacies of the ways propositions of faith have been taught by the magisterium of the Catholic Church. For example, several years ago the theologian Gerald O'Collins wrote in *The Case Against Dogma* that, in the minds of many people, the notion of dogma impinges upon and even denies intellectual freedom. It requires an intellectual sacrifice totally at odds with the way we ordinarily understand things. Prescribed formulations rule out the full play of a free, personal faith when the faithful are obliged by the nature of dogma to internalize dogmatic formulations, even if they do not understand them.

> When the appropriate authorities proclaim a truth as "binding on all the faithful", what are the faithful bound to? Are they required merely to recite a set of words, or at least not to question and deny publicly this set of words? . . . Can we reduce dogmas to the status of public regulations controlling Christian discourse? Dogmas would then become no more than language laws encouraging believers to use certain words (homoousios, transubstantiation, papal infallibility, and so forth), and refrain from using other words (homoiousios, consubstantiation, papal fallibility, and so forth).[8]

If that be the case, he concludes, then despite all appearances of prudent rationality, dogmas demand highly irrational responses.[9] Avery Dulles has pursued some of these themes in a systematic way, situating the discussion of dogma within the post–Vatican II experience of a pluralistic church where changing forms of faith and

[8] Gerald O'Collins, *The Case Against Dogma* (New York: Paulist, 1975), 12.

[9] Nicholas Lash concurs that in "everyday use of the term dogma, an implied element of irrationality and obscurantism" can be found. But rather than attribute this to the nature of dogma itself, Lash attributes this implied irrational element to the legacy of the Enlightenment, which pitted rationalist individualism against tradition and virtually equated tradition with obscurantism. One predictable theological reaction was wariness toward any form of rationalism. See *Change in Focus: A Study of Doctrinal Change and Continuity* (London: Sheed & Ward, 1973), 36. For a discussion of the popular animus against dogma, often undertaken by "pluralists" in a somewhat dogmatic fashion, see W. J. T. Mitchell, "Pluralism as Dogmatism," *Critical Inquiry* 12 (Spring 1986): 494–502.

doubts about the teaching authority of the church have placed in question some traditional notions about dogma.[10] And Francis A. Sullivan has focused primarily upon the nature of dogmatic statements in relation to the teaching authority of the Catholic Church, offering clear criteria for interpreting the various types and levels of church teaching.[11] All of these approaches share a focus on dogma as propositionally expressed and authoritatively taught truth of faith.

The hermeneutics of dogmatic statements has been a special interest of Roman Catholic theologians. One of the most significant studies on this topic, Thomas B. Ommen's *The Hermeneutic of Dogma*, places the problem of dogma within a hermeneutical framework, again focusing on the interpretation of propositions.[12] From the field of biblical studies, Raymond E. Brown has examined the relationship between exegesis and doctrine, focusing on the development of doctrine, or of dogmatic propositions.[13] The hermeneutics of dogma was also addressed by the International Theological Commission in its 1990 document "On the Interpretation of Dogmas."[14] Together with the Pontifical Biblical Commission's 1993 statement on biblical criticism,[15] this constitutes an impressive contribution by the church itself to contemporary discussion about textual hermeneutics, placing dogma within the framework of historical consciousness.[16]

[10] Avery Dulles, *The Survival of Dogma: Faith, Authority, and Dogma in a Changing World* (Garden City, N.Y.: Doubleday, 1973; reprint, New York: Crossroad, 1985).

[11] Francis A. Sullivan, *Magisterium: Teaching Authority in the Catholic Church* (New York: Paulist, 1983); idem, *Creative Fidelity: Weighing and Interpreting Documents of the Magisterium* (New York: Paulist, 1996). Some principles for the interpretation of dogmatic propositions are laid out also by Piet Schoonenberg, "Historicity and the Interpretation of Dogma," *Theology Digest* 18 (1970): 132–43.

[12] Thomas B. Ommen, *The Hermeneutic of Dogma*, dissertation (Missoula, Mont.: Scholars Press, 1975). See also Ommen, "The Hermeneutic of Dogma," *Theological Studies* 35 (1974): 605–31.

[13] Raymond E. Brown, *Biblical Exegesis and Church Doctrine* (New York: Paulist, 1985).

[14] See n. 3 above.

[15] Pontifical Biblical Commission, "The Interpretation of the Bible in the Church," *Origins* 23/29 (January 6, 1994): 497–524.

[16] See Walter Principe, "The Hermeneutic of Roman Catholic Dog-

In addition to these approaches to dogma as propositional or textual matter, two relatively recent studies have focused on the relationship between doctrinal language and the experience of faith. In *Easter in Ordinary*, Roman Catholic theologian Nicholas Lash sees doctrine as an activity of the church through which the church expresses its experience of God.[17] Following the lines of Karl Rahner's theology, he sees doctrinal language (or the dogmatic proposition) not as subsequent expression of the experience but as a constitutive factor in it. Lash is reacting to the highly controversial work of Protestant theologian George A. Lindbeck. In *The Nature of Doctrine* Lindbeck criticizes Rahner's approach and proposes that experience is dependent on the propositions that circumscribe the terrain of faith.[18] I will refer to both of these works in chapters 3 and 4.

From a liberationist perspective, Juan Luis Segundo emphasized the relationship between the need to correlate the concrete, applied life of faith and dogma's function as an articulation of the truth of revelation.[19] According to Segundo, dogma, like the revelation it articulates, is not so much something to be known like an objective datum, as it is something to be experienced in faith. The "truth" of dogmatic formulations is found not in some abstract, "Hellenized" conceptualization but in the evidence that the spirit of Jesus is made manifest in the life of faith, partly through the instrumentality of dogma. The historically specific experience of the church in a particular time and place—for example, the experience of the church in poor Latin American slums—is the place where dogma is born, and where it lives or dies. The great temptation today, Segundo concluded, is to retreat into a dogmatic ghetto where the formulations of the past become meaningless catchphrases, divorced from the contemporary experience of the

matic Statements," *Sciences Religieuses* 2 (1972): 157–75, who describes the possibilities for a fundamentalist use of dogma in the absence of historical consciousness.

[17] Nicholas Lash, *Easter in Ordinary: Reflections on Human Experience and the Knowledge of God* (Charlottesville: University Press of Virginia, 1988).

[18] George A. Lindbeck, *The Nature of Doctrine: Religion and Theology in a Post-Liberal Age* (Philadelphia: Westminster, 1984).

[19] Juan Luis Segundo, *The Liberation of Dogma: Faith, Revelation and Dogmatic Teaching Authority*, trans. Phillip Berryman (Maryknoll, N.Y.: Orbis, 1992).

church. When that divorce occurs, dogma ceases to function in a unifying way.

The intellectual foundations of this study go back to John Henry Newman's seminal work *An Essay on the Development of Christian Doctrine* (1st ed., 1845). The *Essay* resulted from Newman's preoccupation with the continuing viability of the most ancient doctrines of faith. He framed his approach in terms of the organic metaphor of development. Dogma could function as an instrument of unity only if it could be shown to have developed, with the capacity to continue to develop. After Newman, the issue was no longer whether development of unchanging truth could be admitted.[20] Now the issue was exactly how the truth could remain itself even as it really unfolded in the living mind of the church. But Newman also raised another issue. He squarely situated dogmatic development within the history of the church's confession of faith. Dogmatic development was not simply a matter of conceptual maneuvering or logical justification of new definitions of faith taught by the church. It was rather a process within and the result of the church's historical experiences of faith, the entire church's effort to understand the meaning of revelation. Newman broadened dogma beyond propositional matters to include various expressions of the church's confession of faith, especially in liturgical and pietistic practices.

A major task for theology after Newman would be to include as integral to the discussion of dogma the foundational role played by life and experiences of faith found throughout the church. The means by which faith is understood by various sectors of the church, in the process of transmitting it under specific historical circumstances, had to be considered the fundamental context for treating the nature of dogma as a phenomenon reflective of the life of faith in the church. Newman addressed this problem by including in the process of dogmatic development a role for the *consensus fidelium*

---

[20] The facts of change in the force of some dogmas, their gradual decline into desuetude, and actual change in the teaching of the church on some matters lying outside the core of revelation, are indisputable. For an informative historical overview, see Walter Principe, "When 'Authentic' Teachings Change," *The Ecumenist* 25/26 (1987): 70–73, where he offers a list of authentic teachings that have changed in the course of the church's history; and John T. Noonan, Jr., "Development in Moral Doctrine," *Theological Studies* 54 (1993): 662–77.

(the consensus or agreement of the faithful about the content of faith), thus taking into account the legitimacy of local faith responses in contributing to the church's normative dogmatic expressions of faith.

Karl Rahner addressed these issues within the context of one of the great theological developments of the twentieth century, transcendental Thomism. Here the prime analogue was no longer the metaphor of organic development but the faith consciousness of the spiritual subject. Rahner's even-handed treatment of the transcendental faith consciousness of the church, realized in part through the categorical mediations of dogmatic statements, represents a major step toward the retrieval of dogma's unifying function in the church. Here dogmas are seen as "real symbols" of faith that operate between the transcendental faith consciousness of the church and the categorical world within which people actually live their faith. His contribution of the notion of the "collective discovery of truth" pays heed both to Newman's contribution of the *consensus fidelium* and to the contemporary question of joining local interpretations of faith into a larger ecclesial consensus.

The work begun by Newman and furthered by Rahner and others has become ever more pressing as people not previously heard in theological discourse, especially those of women and the poor, attempt to become critically engaged with the dogmatic tradition of faith that addresses them, to interpret and appropriate it, and to offer their own horizons of understanding to the universal church. Hans-Georg Gadamer's philosophical hermeneutics allows for the transmission of elements of tradition in the historically conditioned effort of people to understand traditions by making them their own through dialogue with the classical monuments of traditions. In the "hermeneutical" dialogue, the horizon of a given tradition merges with that of an interlocutor. Not only is a new interpretation given to what is transmitted and received, but the transmitted tradition itself takes on new life. The hermeneutical dialogue generates new authoritative interpretations of the classics of the dogmatic tradition; these interpretations find their source and regulative identity in the transmitted tradition from which they partly derive. The selfsame and authoritative dogmatic tradition rooted in scripture that has always been recognized as such by preceding generations maintains its normative and unifying function, even though new aspects of it may emerge and older ones may be eclipsed by newer ones. In approaching dogma as a classic, the possibility is opened for ongoing interpretation from a variety of angles of faith experience. The notion of the "classic" also offers the flexibility of the ancient *regula fidei* (rule of faith) and finds its anchor in the church's common faith in Jesus Christ, the prime analogue for all dogmatic expressions of faith. This opens the church up to the possibility of some dogmatic change without threatening the revealed core of faith, and of toleration of a variety of theological voices and practices, all finding a consensus of unity of faith rooted in Christ.

In the following chapters I will examine dogma within the frameworks of the developmental model of Newman, the transcendental project of Rahner, and the philosophical hermeneutics of Gadamer. Newman approaches dogma as a supernatural "idea" that impresses itself upon the mind of the church; Rahner approaches it as a mediating symbol of the church's experience of grace; and Gadamer's theory would approach it as an interpreted classic of a tradition transmitted through successive acts of understanding. Each of these approaches contributes a necessary dimension to a comprehensive retrieval of dogma as an instrument of unity.

Newman emphasizes the important dimension of the "immutability" of revealed truth, that what dogma expresses is divine. This is an idea that Rahner elaborates within the framework of his transcendental theology, where he speaks not of the "impression" of the divine "idea" but rather of the self-communication of God in grace to human subjectivity. This self-communication is constant and unchanging, directed to all human beings at all times and places in history. Gadamer, too, is concerned about the issue of the self-sameness of what is transmitted in traditions, but opens up the possibility of a change in the way we come to understand the selfsame content of a transmitted tradition.

Rahner's approach accents the ways in which this revealed truth of what is given in the grace of revelation, the *revelatum,* is mediated to human consciousness. Dogma is understood as a symbolic mediation, a real symbol that expresses the truth of the *revelatum.* This allows for the possibility of a wide range of dogmatic expressions, although the prime analogue remains the dogmatic statement. In this he built upon Newman, who also allowed for a rich variety of modes of dogmatic expression, acknowledging that "dogma" is not only teaching but also confession of faith.

Finally, Gadamer's philosophical hermeneutics offers a framework within which the transmission of a dogmatic tradition can be conceived in such a way as to allow for a pluralism of interpretations around a consensus of understanding. This honors the concern of Newman that the *consensus fidelium* be factored into the teaching of the church, and Rahner's interest in the theological dynamics of the "collective discovery of truth"—how the church as a whole comes to a possession of what God communicates to it.

I shall argue that these three concerns—the integrity of revelation, its various symbolic mediations, and its faithful transmission through a pluralism of interpretations—are necessary parts of a comprehensive grasp of dogma as an instrument of unity rather than of division within a pluralistic church. These concerns in turn direct us toward a unifying criterion for dogma itself, and it is at this point that I will propose the project of a contemporary reappropriation of the ancient *regula fidei*, which is itself rooted in the church's faith in and proclamation of Jesus Christ.

This is an introductory essay. I liken it to the first sketches and primary washes that an artist must make before beginning to apply the paint to the canvas. The layers of texture, depth, color, and contrast that would make for the complete picture will not be found here. Instead, what will be found are the initial and general indications of a more detailed and expansive study that will later on have to address some of the thornier issues raised here, especially those involving ecclesiology and the nature and function of the teaching office. It is my hope that this introductory essay will be of some help to the general reader who is concerned about the challenges to catholic unity that the church now faces.

CHAPTER 1

Dogma and Ecclesial Pluralism

What theological pluralism claims as a matter of principle is that, not simply because of cultural and other differences in the perceiving subject, but also because of the inexhaustible nature of the divine "object", it is impossible to comprehend God from only one viewpoint or to express that comprehension in only one manner.

—John Mahoney[1]

Not so very long ago many, perhaps most, Catholics assumed that dogma meant one thing only: the authoritative doctrine of the Roman magisterium (the teaching authority of the pope) that was handed down to the faithful and simply accepted as a matter of faith. Dogma as teaching of faith was therefore unifying because all Catholics were thought to accept and understand it in the same way, according to the official interpretation of the Catholic Church. In the past thirty years, however, that view has begun to change. The change is centered not on any rejection of the proper role of the teaching authority of the church; indeed, one of the hallmarks of the Roman Catholic Church is that, after two thousand years, popes and bishops continue to teach and interpret the faith with an authority that can only come from the weight of a living tradition. To be a Catholic includes accepting that the authority of this teaching function belongs intrinsically to the nature of the church as instituted by Christ.

What has changed is our understanding of the world of the church: no longer can we understand Catholic unity as the result of the successful imprint of the European form of the church upon the

---

[1] Mahoney, *Making of Moral Theology*, 331.

rest of the world. For example, no one holds that the church in China or the Republic of the Congo has to look like or even function according to all the customs of the church in Italy. There is room for variation according to local needs and customs, a fact to which the history of particular churches (Eastern "rites") within the Catholic communion testifies.[2]

Increasingly, the reassertion of various local forms of faith, shaped by various cultural and intellectual traditions, has led to calls for the acceptance of a certain cultural and even limited theological pluralism within the Catholic Church. For example, in the years following the Second Vatican Council, Latin American theologians were the first to develop the "theology of liberation," an interpretation of the faith tradition that emerged from the particular social, economic, political, and ecclesial realities of Latin America. Unlike most older forms of theology, this theology was explicitly aimed toward social change through a new reading of the scriptures and of the church's own traditions. In time this led to some theological appraisal of the nature of the church itself, especially in light of the church's historic role in the development of the political and economic cultures of Latin America. Gradually priests and lay workers, some with the support of bishops, founded ecclesial base communities (*communidades ecclesiales de base*), which tried to work at the grass roots level to establish a new form of church not limited to the traditional boundaries and operational patterns of diocesan and parish administrative units.

My own brief experience with base communities in Mexico, and later what I witnessed in El Salvador, convinced me not only of the vitality of this approach, but that it would inevitably serve as a source of controversy within the larger church. While, as far as I could see, the central teachings of the Catholic faith were never placed in doubt or jeopardy within these *communidades*, it was clear that some dimensions of faith were accented more than others. For example, sin was understood not only as personal transgression of the law of God but also as the structural injustice engendered by certain political or economic realities. And, without romanticizing poor people or denying their own personal sinfulness, the theology

---

[2] For example, these churches, fully aligned with Rome, nevertheless have always had married clergy.

of liberation tended to emphasize the latter rather than the former type of sin.

In 1984 the Vatican's Congregation for the Doctrine of the Faith issued an "Instruction" on liberation theology that severely criticized this new theology, among other reasons for its approach to sin as a social reality. In contrast to what the Instruction perceived to be a selective presentation of faith by liberation theologians, the Congregation proposed a "full" presentation:

> In this full presentation of Christianity, it is proper to emphasize those essential aspects which the "theologies of liberation" especially tend to misunderstand or to eliminate, namely: the transcendence and gratuity of liberation in Jesus Christ, true God and true man; the sovereignty of grace; and the true nature of the means of salvation, especially of the church and the sacraments. One should also keep in mind the true meaning of ethics, in which the distinction between good and evil is not relativized, the real meaning of sin, the necessity for conversion and the universality of the law of fraternal love.[3]

It did not come as a total surprise that parts of this Instruction were received with puzzlement by some of the people of the local churches who were trying to live their faith according to the principles of a theology of liberation and who did not recognize in the Instruction the theology that had inspired their interpretation of the faith. Despite the validity of many of the points made in this Instruction, some theologians questioned the adequacy of the Instruction for its failure to take into account in a positive fashion the variety of approaches to be found within liberation theology itself. For liberation theology has included a number of different strategies, ranging from the Latin America version to African, African-American, Asian, and even Palestinian liberation projects. In the face of this kind of pluralism, then, the Vatican Instruction

---

[3] Congregation for the Doctrine of the Faith, "Instruction on Certain Aspects of the 'Theology of Liberation,'" *Origins* 14/13 (September 13, 1984): 193–204, at 104. For a discussion of the Vatican's reception of liberation theology and an interpretation of the 1984 Instruction, see Roger Haight, *An Alternate Vision: An Interpretation of Liberation Theology* (New York: Paulist, 1985); and Arthur F. McGovern, *Liberation Theology and Its Critics: Towards an Assessment* (Maryknoll, N.Y.: Orbis, 1989).

served as a note not so much of unity as of discord—a generic criticism of a pluriform reality.[4]

In light of this kind of experience, we need to ask: How can we recover a sense of dogma, even in the ordinary sense of a Vatican Instruction, such that it might unify rather than divide? How can dogma be understood in such a way that, while expressing the normative understanding of faith, it also admits of a pluralism of interpretive perspectives without compromising the unity of the church? In order to locate such a unifying function for dogma, we must first undertake an appraisal of dogma itself and consider whether the usual understanding of dogma and its functions is adequate to the problems raised by ecclesial pluralism. This calls, first, for an overview of the term "dogma" and some understanding of its development into our current understanding of it as authoritative church teaching. I will suggest that this understanding of dogma constitutes a narrowing of the richness of dogma, which has functioned like a mediation of the confession of faith as much as a body of teaching in the life of the church. I then turn to the life of the contemporary Catholic Church and focus on one note of it, pluralism in the forms of faith confession. This ecclesial pluralism provides the context within which the function of dogma must be understood.

FROM CONFESSION TO TEACHING

"Dogma" is a multivalent term, and this fact complicates any approach to it. For most people, dogma immediately denotes a dogmatic teaching, an authoritatively taught statement of the truth of divine revelation. In this understanding, dogmas comprise the few infallible teachings of popes and councils, those teachings of the church that are substantially dependent on revelation for their authenticity, and the teachings of the ordinary magisterium of the church. But dogma understood as this kind of church teaching

---

[4] Indeed, so strong was the reaction against it that this first Instruction was followed a few months later by a clarification that attempted a more affirmative approach to some of the insights of liberation theology. See Congregation for the Doctrine of the Faith, "Instruction on Christian Freedom and Liberation," *Origins* 15/44 (April 17, 1986): 713-28.

(doctrine in any form) is only the most recent rendering of the term. Dogma can also be understood more broadly as a confessional "theme" that runs through the life of faith, that which pertains to *fides qua*, how faith is confessed, as distinguished from *fides quae*, the "content" of belief. As we shall see below, in its earlier and broader meaning it included the various expressions of the life of faith that constitute a living tradition, specifically creedal formulations, liturgy, and ecclesiastical disciplines such as priestly celibacy, as well as some of the theological traditions that emerged from local churches. One can distinguish, then, between dogmas properly so-called (the particular teachings of faith) and the dogma of the church (the whole complexus of faith constituted by the various elements of the faith tradition). It is this latter, broader notion that I wish to keep in mind here, the notion that dogma is not only propositionally taught matter, but rather, that it is also thematic of the church's life of faith. This life of faith is articulated not only in propositions but also in the rich heritage of "dogmatic" signs, symbols, practices, and theological traditions that together constitute the confession of faith.

Without conflating "dogma" with "doctrine," one might nevertheless find some help in understanding the richness of the term "dogma" by turning to the definition of "doctrine" offered by the distinguished church historian Jaroslav Pelikan. Doctrine is usually taken to mean the content of faith (the *fides quae*) as expressed in church teaching . But Pelikan expands the term to include other dimensions of the life of faith (the *fides qua*). For Pelikan, doctrine comprises "what the church believes, confesses and teaches, based on the Word of God."[5] What Pelikan claims for doctrine we could claim also for dogma, establishing it as a much wider notion than the one Catholics (and post-Enlightenment culture in general) often presume. Let us take a closer look at what Pelikan means by belief, confession, and teaching.

The source of doctrine is the "Word of God," God's revelation in Jesus Christ, understood as God's self-communication within history and mediated in the word of scripture and the traditions of faith, for example, the Nicene Creed. *Belief* includes those creeds

---

[5] Jaroslav Pelikan, *The Christian Tradition: A History of the Development of Doctrine*, vol. 1, *The Emergence of the Catholic Tradition (100-600)* (Chicago: University of Chicago Press, 1971), 1.

and other symbols of faith that articulate faith. These are often expressed through sacramental traditions and through the various theologies that interpret them. *Confession* involves those liturgical practices and modes of pietistic and spiritual practice by which one ritualizes and articulates this faith, for example, the liturgy. *Teaching* includes doctrines of various degrees of authority, the teachings of councils, and solemnly defined authoritatively taught "dogmas" in the modern sense of the term. For our purposes here, we can say that dogma as a theme includes not only the teaching of the church but also the various modes of the church's confession of faith, and the interplay between the two, especially in liturgical, disciplinary, and theological traditions.

Dogma as a theme of both teaching and confession of faith is not a new notion. The great Dominican theologian Yves Congar established in his groundbreaking work on tradition that in the earliest days of the church "dogma" was expressed not only verbally but also sacramentally. Both eucharist and baptism were vehicles for confession of faith, long before the theological interpretation of these rituals led to authoritative "dogmatic" statements about them. Early theological speculation was not abstracted from liturgy: it derived from the sense of faith within the church that came to expression in the liturgy.

> [W]hen one studies the theology of baptism according to the Fathers of the second century, one finds little reference to the writings of St. Paul. Nevertheless a doctrine is elaborated essentially beginning with [*à partir de*] the reality of baptism itself, as held and lived within the Church. One could well say, and in so saying, one would define the inspiration [*génie*] itself of the Fathers and of the liturgy: a doctrine simply expresses the meaning of that which is done within the Church.[6]

The rich symbolism of the baptismal liturgy provided a ready link between the confession and the teaching of faith, illustrating the ancient maxim *lex orandi lex credendi* (the law of prayer is the law of

[6] Yves M.-J. Congar, *La Tradition et les traditions*, vol. 2, *Essai théologique* (Paris: Arthème Fayard, 1963), 116. This book is the companion volume to *La Tradition et les traditions*, vol. 1, *Essai historique* (Paris: Arthème Fayard, 1960). I have consulted and emended the English translation, *Tradition and Traditions: An Historical and a Theological Essay*, trans. Michael Naseby and Thomas Rainborough (New York: Macmillan, 1966), 354.

belief), a maxim that rooted the church's articulated belief in its worship.[7] Like the trinitarian doxologies that can be traced to the very first decades of the church, the baptismal formulae contained in capsule form an entire theological treatise that would take centuries to elaborate, expressed for the time being as a simple but comprehensive confession of faith. Even the act of immersion in the baptismal waters constituted a form of "dogmatic" instruction with a message of death to sin and birth in a new life in Christ, and this message was plain to all the witnesses.

Dogmatic teaching is therefore but one part of the whole dogmatic complexus of faith. It stands in intimate relationship with the articulation of the confession of faith in liturgy and church practices, and the theological interpretation of the content of faith. The use of the term "dogma" is therefore too narrow when it denominates almost exclusively official church teaching. However, in recent times, not only church officials but also many systematic theologians have presumed such a restricted definition of the term. According to that understanding, dogma is "a divinely revealed truth, proclaimed as such by the infallible teaching authority of the church, and hence binding on all the faithful without exception, now and forever."[8] Dogma thus denotes a linguistic expression of divinely revealed truth, and the truth itself, so expressed. As we shall see, the problem with this definition is that in its exclusive focus on propositional expression of the truth, it risks abstracting dogma from the historically conditioned life of faith in the church, from the church's confession of faith that takes place in many times, places, and modalities. Dogma becomes less a theme and more exclusively a linguistic phenomenon to be decoded, interpreted, or explained.

This is not to deny, as Heinrich Fries has noted (following Gerhard Ebeling), that dogma is a kind of "speech event." That is, it intends to communicate information about the content and mean-

---

[7] Antonius Brekelmans, "Professions de Foi dans l'église primitive: origine et fonction," *Concilium* (Paris) 51 (1970): 39.

[8] Dulles, *Survival of Dogma*, 156. E. Dublanchy's approach is similar, identifying dogma itself with the truth it articulates: "Following Catholic teaching, dogma is a truth revealed by God and is as such directly proposed by the Church for our belief" (my translation). See "Dogme," *Dictionnaire de théologie catholique* (Paris: Letouzey, 1923–1972), 4: 1575.

ing of faith itself.[9] As such, it has the character of a speaker in relation to a hearer, one who in speaking makes a claim, even binds the hearer in some way. This is as true for creedal symbols, liturgical modes of confession, and ecclesiastical disciplines as it is for the ordinary church teaching on faith and morals given by popes and bishops. Furthermore, all dogmatic expressions of faith are historically conditioned and stand within a history of faith that continues to shape them. Because of this, dogma as confession of faith stands as a sign of the historical shape of faith itself.[10] But taken only as a proposition, dogma can seem to occupy an empyrean stratum of truth that has no necessary connection to the historical contexts within which faith is lived. Because it is thought to express unchanging verities, it thereby shares itself in the aura of that unchangeability. Yet this notion of dogma strays significantly from the understanding of the early church, where dogma was the articulation of the confession of the catholic faith through a number of channels, especially the liturgy and early creeds. Only gradually did it come to be identified with the ordinary teaching of the church, especially by popes and bishops. In fact, the gradual rise of this notion of dogma corresponded to the consolidation of the church's teaching authority into the Roman magisterium. It would be helpful at this juncture to trace the lines of this massively important transformation.

Early Uses of "Dogma" as Confession

The word "dogma" can be traced to the Greek infinitive *dokein*, meaning "to seem." The very earliest usages of the word "dogma" refer to a stated civic belief, an articulated focal point for consensus about what is agreeable or seemly to all. As early as Plato's *Sophist* and *Laws*, however, we find a linkage between dogma and theological belief. In the *Sophist* (265C), *ta dedogmena* refers to possible opinions about the creation of the world. In the *Laws* (887E–888D)

---

[9] Heinrich Fries, *Fundamental Theology*, trans. Robert J. Daly (Washington, D.C.: Catholic University of America, 1996), 54, 105–8.

[10] Ibid., 96. See also Schoonenberg, "Historicity and the Interpretation of Dogma," 132–43, who argues that "dogma is situated in history and is determined by it."

dogma refers to correct belief about the gods. In both cases, though, the primary meaning is much closer to correct theological opinion than to an authoritatively taught tenet. The correct opinion often remained unwritten, the province of a philosophical school or the object of philosophical discourse.[11] It was, however, but a brief step from these quasi-theological usages to the investment of "dogma" with the authority of a public and official belief or teaching.[12]

In the New Testament the word "dogma" rarely appears, but when it does it refers to a decree of some kind. A direct connection between the New Testament usage and early ecclesiastical usage of the word is difficult to establish.[13] In Luke 2:1 and Acts 17:7, dogma refers to a royal edict or proscription. In Ephesians and Colossians, it refers to the claims of the Mosaic law.[14] In Acts 16:4 dogma more closely anticipates modern usage, as it seems to refer to the deci-

[11] H. P. Owen, "Dogma," *Encyclopedia of Philosophy* (New York: Macmillan, 1967), 2:10. But see Rudolf Kittel, *"dogma," Theological Dictionary of the New Testament*, trans. and ed. Geoffrey W. Bromiley (Grand Rapids, Mich.: Eerdmans, 1964), 2:230–31. Kittel argues that early usages of the word "dogma" refer to that which seems good to an individual person or to an assembly. But many early attestations, including religious ones, refer to authoritative civic decrees or authoritative tenets of philosophical schools. With this Kittel seems to agree. As an example, he points to the Torah, which becomes in later Judaism a system comparable to the *dogmata* of philosophy: a repository of the principles of divine philosophy that is both studied and taught. Kasper argues that these early usages leave open much room for peculiarly subjective understandings of commonly held tenets. See *Dogma unter dem Wort Gottes*, 30–31.

[12] See Dublanchy, "Dogme," *Dictionnaire de théologie catholique*, 4:1574: "The word dogma, from *dókeo*, signifies from its etymology and habitual usage by the Greeks not only an opinion which seemed founded or which one preferred, but also a formal and well devised [*arretée*] resolution, such as a decree or a law" (my translation).

[13] See Kasper, *Dogma unter dem Wort Gottes*, 28: "The New Testament hardly knows the word dogma [*dógma*], and certainly does not use it in the contemporary theological sense" (my translation).

[14] "In those days a decree [*dogma*] went out" (Luke 2:1); "they are all acting against the decrees of Caesar [*tōn dogmatōn Kaisaros*]"(Acts 17:7); "by abolishing in his flesh the law of commandments and ordinances [*dogmasin*]" (Eph. 2:15); "having canceled the bond which stood against us with its legal demands [*dogmasin*]" (Col. 2:14).

sions of the Council of Jerusalem, which issued a decree on dietary regulations and on the issue of circumcision.[15]

The evidence suggests that no single meaning of the term was fixed very early in the life of the church. The post-apostolic fathers used the word to refer not only to the teachings and ethical prescriptions of Jesus, but, negatively and polemically, even to the false teachings of the heretics.[16] Dogma functioned not only to help the church to define itself over and against other religions and theologies but also as a mediating locus for church unity:

> The various teachings of the Apostles and the different liturgical practices of the churches pressed for unification and synthesis, not only with each other, but also with the Jewish and Hellenic environment. This unification, however, could only be achieved through generally valid formulations of what was to count as "correct" teaching, i.e., orthodoxy. Dogmas as a means of unification arose immediately out of the universal claim of the proclamation itself.[17]

It is this synthetic, unifying function of dogma as both universal teaching and universal practice, though subject to local interpretation, that is at stake today. If that unifying function has been lost to modern consciousness, it can be regained partly through a retrieval of a sense of the richness of dogma, which originally extended beyond authoritatively taught propositions understood in only one way to an array of faith expressions, especially liturgical symbols, church disciplines, and particular theologies that could, in their commonality and difference, represent a rich variety of interpretations of the content of faith. For various reasons, the richness of

[15] "[T]hey delivered to them for observance the decisions [*ta dogmata*] which had been reached by the apostles and elders at Jerusalem" (Acts 16:4). Kasper holds that this usage in Acts constitutes only a venerable foreshadowing of the modern understanding of dogma as an authoritative pronouncement of the church on matters of faith and morals. *Dogma unter dem Wort Gottes*, 29.

[16] Ibid., 31–32; Kittel, "*dogma*," 231–32. As late as 649, dogma was used by the Roman synod at the Lateran in reference to heresy.

[17] David Krieger, *The New Universalism: Foundations for a Global Theology* (Maryknoll, N.Y.: Orbis, 1991), 18–19. This was true of the creeds as well. Fries notes that creeds have functioned (1) to distinguish faith from what it is not, and (2) to indicate the universality of faith by bringing to expression what can be included in this faith.

dogma as a theme in the church's life was narrowed to authoritative church teaching.

We have seen that the process of verbal formalization of faith began with the creedal statements that were contained within the baptismal liturgies. Like the apostolic teachings, the early creeds functioned in two ways: as a mediation of faith to culture through an articulation of belief, and, through this articulation of belief as an expression of the confession of faith, that is, an expression of praise—doxology.[18] The Niceno-Constantinopolitan Creed reflects an advanced stage of this creedal linkage between confession and teaching, but like the early creeds, it joins in a doctrinal formulation the expression of both belief (*pistis*) and of praise (*doxa*). How, then, did dogma become almost exclusively associated with church teaching?

Emergence of "Dogma" as Teaching

The Council of Chalcedon (451) marked the point where this intrinsic linkage between belief and praise was broken by the departure from the language of confession ("We believe . . .") in favor of the language of teaching ("We hold and teach to be true . . .").[19] In fact, the development of this distinction between confession and teaching was the result of a very gradual process of narrowing of dogma as both confession and teaching into the authoritative teaching of the hierarchical magisterium. This process can be attributed to historical factors that converged in the centuries following the Council of Trent (1545–1563) but which had their origins long before Trent. Lash argues that the reforms initiated in the eleventh century by Pope Gregory VII (Hildebrand) resulted in "a shrinkage in the notion of the church" from the idea of "the whole community" to the clergy alone. Simultaneously, "the concept of ecclesiastical authority as that of the exercise of a ministry through whose activ-

---

[18] Lash speaks of "[t]he need of christian faith to situate itself—positively or negatively, affirmatively or polemically—in relation to the human culture and society in which it lives. [And] on the other hand, the need of christian faith to express its praise of and trust in God" (*Change in Focus*, 47).

[19] Kasper, *Dogma unter dem Wort Gottes*, 48.

ity God is present to his people was gradually supplanted by a concept of personally possessed power and authority."[20] Congar adds that by the Middle Ages the old idea was fading that the bishops, by their agreement, were the revealers of a doctrine that had always been held as part of the rule of faith or deposit of faith. This was being replaced by the notion that God directly inspires popes, bishops, and councils, in a top-down vertical fashion, as to the meaning of revelation and its implications for the church's institutional life.[21] This view was buttressed by what Lash calls "a theology of church structures with the hierarchy the focus of attention." The "transmitting organism" of the faith tradition came to be seen "not as the church as a whole, but as the ecclesiastical hierarchy."[22]

Congar and others traced this development to a number of factors. Among them are the traditional and legitimate claims of the See of Rome to primacy, which begins early in the second century; various reassertions of these claims in the ninth and eleventh centuries; the great reform movements of Leo IX and Gregory VII that increased papal authority and power and sanctioned a juridical approach to ecclesiology and church teaching; the rise of anti-ecclesiastical sects from the twelfth century onward which provoked the development of papal prerogative; theological disputes which raised among canonists many issues concerning theological criteria for determining the content of faith and resulted in growth in legalistic thinking; the growing view, promoted by Boniface VIII, that the pope was above the law and that he could change the law of the church; the development of the notion of authority itself, especially the modern theory of sovereignty, which took on a new absolutist form in which communities were rigorously subjected to their head;

---

[20] Lash, *Change in Focus*, 41. See R. W. Southern, *Western Society and the Church in the Middle Ages*, vol. 2 of *The Pelican History of the Church* (Baltimore: Penguin, 1970), 34–44, 100–6, 181.

[21] Congar adds: "Such is the position of Irenaeus, such also that of Vincent of Lerins. It is in this line [of thinking] that, for ten centuries, popes, bishops, councils, canonists, and theologians have not ceased to affirm that the role of hierarchical persons is to guard and to apply the laws received and transmitted; the deposit of faith, the dogmas and the canons of the councils, the received tradition of the Fathers." *La Tradition et les traditions*, vol. 1, *Essai historique*, 233–34 (my translation).

[22] Lash, *Change in Focus*, 41.

and the growing rift between the church and the secular world, which required the intervention of the doctrinal authority of the church.[23]

This consolidation of tradition and of the teaching authority of the church into the hierarchical magisterium coincided with the abstraction of dogmatic teaching from the church's ordinary confession of faith—an abstraction reflected in the very usage of the word "dogma" during this long period of transition. We have already noted that the word was not used with absolute consistency in the primitive church. Nor did it command great attention in the medieval church or its theology.[24] Thomas Aquinas hardly uses it at all in the *Summa theologiae*. He relies instead on the term *articulus fidei* (article of faith) to refer to those beliefs that must be distinguished from one another in the mind of the believer.[25] The *articulus fidei* is not merely a doctrinal assertion; it is an expression of the confession of faith. Thus, Aquinas holds that it is appropriate that the *articuli fidei* be converted into or used as creedal formulations or symbols of faith.[26] The *articulus fidei* implies an identification in one doctrinal statement of both teaching and confession of the central mysteries of revelation.[27] It emphasizes both the

[23] Congar, *La Tradition et les traditions*, vol. 1, *Essai historique*, 235–37. See also the more recent work by J. M. R. Tillard, *The Bishop of Rome*, trans. John de Satgé (Wilmington, Del.: Michael Glazier, 1983), which traces the process of the identification of church teaching with the personal infallibility of the pope. See also Mahoney, *Making of Moral Theology*, 118–19, on the decisive rejection of the conciliar teaching of the Council of Constance (1414–1418) by Pope Martin V and his successors.

[24] Kasper, *Dogma unter dem Wort Gottes*, 34.

[25] *Summa theologiae*, 2-2, 1, 6: "Now the perception of the divine truth comes to us by way of distinction [*distinctionem*]; for those things which are one in God are multiplied [*multiplicantur*] in our intellect. Therefore what is believed [*credibilia*] should be distinguished by articles. . . . Accordingly articles of faith are to be distinguished" (my translation).

[26] *Summa theologiae* 2-2, 1, 9: "And thus it was necessary that the truths of faith be collected together as one [*in unum colligi*] in order that it might more easily be proposed to all. . . . And it is from this kind of collection of the sayings [*sententiarum*] of faith that the name 'symbol' has been found appropriate [*acceptum est*]" (my translation).

[27] "Even when, as we have seen, the concept of an 'article of faith' came also to refer to propositions other than those contained in the Apostles'

church's sense of faith (*sensus fidei*) and the rational interpretation of the content of revelation. Some argue that it is this latter, rational element that potentially allowed for an abstraction of the dogmatic teaching of faith from the language of confession and praise.[28] In any case, the connection between teaching and confession achieved in the *articulus fidei* became the chief characteristic of the occasional medieval usage of the word "dogma" itself.[29]

The theological basis for a connection between teaching of the church and confession of the faithful was gradually lost as the need for an authoritative interpretation of the church's confession of faith grew more pressing, especially after the Reformation, and during the Enlightenment. On what basis was the confession of faith to be interpreted and established as normative? Long after the Council of Trent the Franciscan theologian Philipp Neri Chrismann

---

Creed, the link between the two was maintained. Only those propositions are referred to as 'articles of faith' which express fundamental aspects of revealed truth not reducible to some other element in the content of tradition. Thus in sharp contrast to the usage with which we have become familiar in modern times, for medieval theology the criterion according to which a doctrinal statement was classified as an 'article of faith' was the centrality of its content in the christian mystery as a whole." Lash, *Change in Focus*, 51.

[28] See Lash, *Change in Focus*, 52: "There occurred in medieval theology a shift of emphasis from the personal and religious to the theoretical and 'scientific'. Because, in Lonergan's words, 'the sharp opposition between the two realms of meaning' was not 'adequately grasped', the seeds were sown both of that rationalism in theology which infected the eighteenth and nineteenth centuries and of the various forms of pietism and pragmatism which were its inevitable antithesis."

[29] The hymn for Corpus Christi, *"Lauda Sion Salvatorem,"* traditionally attributed to Thomas Aquinas, reflects just such a connection between what the faithful confess and what is authoritatively given to Christians as the teaching of faith: "Dogma datur christianis/quod in carnem transit panis/et vinum in sanguinem" (It is a dogma given to Christians that bread passes over into flesh and wine into blood). See Kasper, *Dogma unter dem Wort Gottes*, 34. The hymn stresses the doctrinal element of the article of faith, but it is composed precisely as a liturgical hymn whose purpose is confessional. Kasper cites M. Elze, "Der Begriff des Dogmas in der Alten Kirche," *Zeitschrift für Theologie und Kirche* 61 (1964): 437, who finds Thomas's usage of the word "dogma" here "to manifest an almost poetic freedom" (my translation).

(1751–1810) was to offer an answer: clarify and harden Trent's usage of the term "dogma." But the Council of Trent had not been utterly clear about the meaning of dogma, or where dogma stood in relation to the overarching tradition of faith. In his famous study of Trent, Hubert Jedin judged that an ambiguity between the "dogmatic" and "disciplinary" notions of tradition colored those early sessions during which the program of the council was being established. The dogmatic notion of tradition included all the teaching derived from scripture, the creeds, and apostolic writings, while the disciplinary notion included religious practices, some of which, such as the sign of the cross and infant baptism, found partial warrant in apostolic sources.[30] In his *Regula fidei Catholicae* (1792), Chrismann leaned toward the "dogmatic" notion of tradition and limited the meaning of dogma to those solemn definitions of faith given in official church teachings which were held by all in the world to be divinely revealed. If the truth of dogma were to be received by the church universal, it would be received on the basis of the universal claim of the church's teaching authority, exercised in the promulgation of dogmatic propositions with the weight of law.[31]

It is no small coincidence that while this shift was taking place at rather theoretical levels, the institutionalization of the teaching function of the church as the Roman magisterium was accelerating. While the word "magisterium" was not even used by the Council of Trent, the Post-Reformation period saw the contraction of the concept of tradition "until it was virtually identified with one of the

---

[30] Hubert Jedin, *A History of the Council of Trent*, trans. E. Graf (St. Louis, Mo.: Herder, 1961), 2:62–63. See also Maurice Bévenot, "*Traditiones* in the Council of Trent," *Heythrop Journal* 4 (1963): 333–47.

[31] See Philipp Neri Chrismann, *Regula fidei Catholicae et collectio dogmatum credendorum* (Wirceburgi: Stahelianis, 1854), nos. 5–40. Chrismann declares: "A dogma of faith is nothing other than a divinely revealed doctrine and truth which by the judgment of the church is proposed for belief as a matter of divine faith, such that anything proposed contrary to the church should be condemned as heretical doctrine" (my translation). Kasper notes that although the *Regula fidei Catholicae* was placed on the Index in 1868 because of its minimalistic tendencies, it was nevertheless virtually adopted word for word by Vatican I, Pius IX's *Syllabus of Errors*, *Pascendi*, the *Syllabus* of Pius X, and *Munificentissimus Deus*. See *Dogma unter dem Wort Gottes*, 36–37.

organs of tradition: namely, the episcopate and, especially, the papacy."[32] Dogma had come to be identified with official church teaching from popes or councils about faith and morals, the latter understood in the sense of teaching the moral implications of faith.

This final refinement reached its apogee in the nineteenth century, when the church's teaching authority, or magisterium, became almost exclusively identified with the pope and bishops. Lash explains:

> Although the distinction between "the teaching church" and "the taught church" was by now firmly established, the term magisterium was still being consistently used to refer to a function in the church. At some point in the mid-nineteenth century, the term began to be used to refer also, and eventually exclusively, to a particular group of functionaries in the church: the pope and other bishops. . . . In view of this shift in meaning and of the survival of "vertical contact" models of the relationship between God and ecclesiastical office-holders, it is not difficult to see how the assumption could emerge that such officeholders could appeal to a "special assistance" of the Holy Spirit as a sufficient warrant for their pronouncements and decisions.[33]

The First Vatican Council (1869–1870) ratified this entire trend. In the teaching of this council, dogma refers to those infallible declarations of the pope pertaining to faith or morals, distinguished from the content or deposit of revelation itself, which are valid and truthful *ex sese* (of themselves), with regard to their intrinsic truth and not with regard to the explicit consent of church members.[34]

---

[32] Lash, *Change in Focus*, 75.

[33] Ibid. The narrowing of the term "dogma" is thus directly related to the narrowing of the teaching function of the church, and even more perilously, as Congar suggests, "to Denzinger." See Congar, *La Tradition et les traditions,* vol. 2, *Essai théologique,* 298 n. 95.

[34] First Vatican Council, *Pastor Aeternis (Constitutio dogmatica prima de ecclesia Christi),* chapter 4, in *Decrees of the Ecumenical Councils,* 2 vols., ed. Norman Tanner (New York: Sheed & Ward and Georgetown, 1990), 2:816 (DS 3074). [The "DS" numbers following conciliar citations refer to those found in Heinrich Denziger, *Enchiridion symbolorum definitionum et declarationum de rebus fidei et morum,* 37th ed., ed. Peter Hünermann (Freiburg: Herder, 1991)]. For commentary, see Lash, *Change in Focus,* 56; and Kasper, *Dogma unter dem Wort Gottes,* 130–31. Lash notes that this had the

This set the stage for the contemporary ecclesiastical usage of the word "dogma." The language of confession and of teaching, which the earlier creedal formulations and the notion of the *articulus fidei* had connected in one statement, could now be formally distinguished. Yet it was the very unity of confession and teaching in a single expression of faith, doctrinal or liturgical, that had originally endowed dogma with a unifying function.

The Abstraction of Dogma as Propositional Truth

This consolidation of the church's teaching authority into the hierarchical magisterium meant that dogma itself came to be perceived as a body of abstract truth transcending ordinary human experience, often at variance with the way people ordinarily understood the world. It gradually ceased to serve as an instrument of the mediation of faith within culture, and instead often seemed to assert itself against culture. Something that was of itself irreformable could not readily engage a post-Enlightenment world increasingly open to the revolutions taking place in epistemology and science, as well as the developments in the understanding of the human person as a free being endowed with "rights."

And, as dogma became abstracted from culture, it also became abstracted from the confessions of faith that take place within cultural situations, and even from a consultation of the *sensus fidelium* (faith sense of the faithful) of the church.[35] As it thus became limited to propositions taught by the Roman magisterium, it became hypostatized as a linguistic phenomenon virtually immune to change.

------

ironic effect of raising the question of the way in which dogmas share in the immutability of revealed truth.

[35] However, some "consultation" of the *sensus fidelium* was thought necessary even before the First Vatican Council. Newman, for example, recounts the work of Father Giovanni Perrone, S.J., on the role played by the "consultation" of the *sensus fidelium* in the 1854 definition of the Immaculate Conception. Newman, *On Consulting the Faithful in Matters of Doctrine*, ed. John Coulson (London: Geoffrey Chapman, 1961), 62–73. Specific methods of "consultation" were used in conjunction with the declaration of the Assumption of Mary by Pope Pius XII in 1950. See chapter 2 for a discussion of this principle in Newman's thought.

Thus did dogmas come to be seen as purely propositional matter abstracted from the living contexts of faith out of which they arose. Such a perception of dogma has become normal, so that people often think that dogmas actually "champion a reality that is, or professes to be, independent of and separable from their historical genesis."[36] Yet, as Fries suggests, it is the human person, a real historical being, who is addressed by divine revelation as a "you." Propositions of truths are grounded in faith as trust, in personal relation, between God and the human addressees of revelation.[37] If we lose sight of this fundamental point, then faith, and the dogmatic elements of the faith tradition that carry it through history, can dissolve into ideology. The abstraction of dogma from the life of faith can result in a naive, uncritical, and even uncomprehending identification of propositions with the full truth of revelation. We are then left with what Jürgen Habermas has called "pure theory," which, "wanting to derive everything from itself . . . succumbs to unacknowledged external conditions and becomes ideological."[38]

This brief rehearsal of the history of the term opens up a new dimension of the problem with dogma in the contemporary church. Dogma's abstraction from the living, historical contexts within which people confess and practice their faith results in a notion of dogma that is impervious to change and thus unable to address the people of faith who live within changing cultural situations. Related to this is the tendency to view dogma as a teaching imposed from above, apart from "a lived understanding" of it through its reception and appropriation by local churches.[39] If dogmatic teaching is neither "received" nor appropriated, and is viewed as abstract and unadaptable to concrete human reality, then it cannot readily function as an instrument of ecclesial unity in a culturally pluralistic context. If dogma is to play a unifying function within the church, then we must ask how it can express the truth of

[36] Werner Elert, *Die Kirche und ihre Dogmengeschichte* (Munich: Evangelischer Presseverband, 1950), 3, as cited by Jaroslav Pelikan, *Historical Theology: Continuity and Change in Christian Doctrine* (London: Hutchinson, 1971), xiv.

[37] Fries, *Fundamental Theology,* 14–16.

[38] Jürgen Habermas, *Knowledge and Human Interests,* trans. Jeremy J. Shapiro (Boston: Beacon, 1971), 314–16.

[39] Kasper, *Dogma unter dem Wort Gottes,* 42. On the importance of "reception theory" in the post-conciliar understanding of incorporation

faith, as faith is realized in the particularity of local church situations, in such a way as to safeguard the unity of faith itself. This leads to a consideration of the pluralistic context of the contemporary church.

THE PROBLEM OF PLURALISM AND CATHOLICITY

The pluralism of faith expressions in liturgy, practice, theology, and even local church teaching evident within the Catholic church today is one of the hallmarks of Catholicism. It is a fact that the church as a whole cannot evade in the name of unity. As Werner Jeanrond, one of the leading contributors to hermeneutical theory in Catholic theology, has observed: "Different people have witnessed to the original Christ event in very different communities, times, and linguistic and cultural contexts. Accepting this pluralism is a necessity for every Christian and not just an option reserved for critical theologians."[40] But pluralism has often made it difficult to articulate a normative dogmatic rendering of the one faith for the entire world. Much of the early history of the church, especially the first great councils, was an attempt to do this within the context of the Mediterranean world and the declining Roman empire. The challenge of achieving unity within diversity, or of reconciling the one faith to its many local and very particular cultural expressions, is in fact an ancient challenge that ties the present situation to past ages of the church.

The New Testament itself attests to a multiplicity of teachings about Jesus Christ and a simultaneous fundamental unity in the identification of the human Jesus with the risen Lord.[41] Congar and

---

of the local churches in the teaching of the Second Vatican Council, see Michael Himes, "The Ecclesiological Significance of Reception of Doctrine," *Heythrop Journal* 33 (1992): 146–60. For a focus on reception in one of the local churches, that of Latin America, see J. Miguez Bonino, "The Reception of Vatican II in Latin America," *Ecumenical Review* 37 (1985): 266–74.

[40] Werner G. Jeanrond, *Theological Hermeneutics: Development and Significance* (New York: Crossroad, 1991), 175–76.

[41] See James D. G. Dunn, *Unity and Diversity in the New Testament: An Inquiry into the Character of Earliest Christianity*, 2d ed. (London: SCM,

others have demonstrated convincingly how beyond the New Testament era a diversity of customs and opinions was widely recognized, especially in the Eastern church, as essentially compatible with the unity of faith. The movement toward uniformity of doctrine and practice was only the result of a very long and gradual process of growth in Roman prestige, a process that culminated only after the sixth century.[42] The search for a more precise creedal and doctrinal agreement was an attempt to distinguish the universal faith from particular theologies and heresies, and to help bring about a catholic consensus as the church expanded into and beyond the Mediterranean theater.

The Meanings of "Catholicity"

Pluralism has not always been easily accepted or assimilated by the church, and "catholicity" has taken on different meanings.[43] On the one hand, catholicity denotes commonality of doctrine (e.g., creedal agreement) and practice (e.g., the common celebration of Christmas—though not Easter) throughout the Christian world. The stress here is on uniform order within the world of faith, giving rise to a universal church of uniform doctrine and practice. We can call this the "universalist" model. On the other hand, catholicity denotes a communion of particular churches emerging from con-

---

1990), 226–28; and Brown, *Biblical Exegesis and Church Doctrine*, especially chapter 7, pp. 123–26.

[42] See Congar's exhaustive treatment of this issue in *Diversity and Communion*, trans. John Bowden (Mystic, Conn.: Twenty-Third, 1985), 23–33. Congar held that popes Damasus, Siricius, and Innocent I, in the fourth and fifth centuries, began "to identify unity of discipline with unity of faith and then to interpret unity in terms of uniformity" (p. 29). However, Robert Eno maintains that even with the rise of Leo and Gelasius, and the foundation of Roman preeminence among the churches, automatic obedience to Rome was not presupposed. See Eno, *The Rise of the Papacy* (Wilmington, Del.: Michael Glazier, 1990).

[43] For a discussion of pluralism within the theology of the church, see International Theological Commission, *El Pluralismo teológico* (Madrid: Biblioteca de Autores Cristianos, 1976). For discussion of the implications of pluralism for ethics and moral theory, see Jacques Pohier, ed., *Christian Ethics: Uniformity, Universality, Pluralism* (New York: Seabury, 1981).

sensus about the essential core of faith.[44] Here the stress lies on that unity that emerges from a commonly shared life in the Spirit among the local churches that together constitute and instantiate the one church catholic. We can call this the "communion" model. While these are not mutually exclusive models, they are substantially different in what they emphasize and in how they approach the pluralism to be found within the church.

The centralization of authority under the bishop by Ignatius of Antioch was in part a reaction to a disconcerting pluralism within the Mediterranean churches, especially the proliferation of various forms of Gnosticism that Ignatius personally witnessed.[45] For Ignatius, the solution to the problem of pluralism was a catholicity of church order in dogmatic teaching and the practice of faith. This would result in a uniformity of practice throughout the geographic world of faith, the adoption of a universalist model of catholicity. Gradually, the guarantee for this kind of universality came through the authority of bishops, particularly the bishop of Rome. By the time of Leo and Gelasius, in the fifth century, Rome claimed "the final and definitive word in the church," thus guaranteeing a geographically realized catholicity of faith.[46] On the other hand, Augustine, in the face of the threatening divisiveness of Donatism, understood catholicity to be constituted by the current consent by all people of the church everywhere (not only the bishops) about what constituted the truth of faith.[47] His was closer to a model of

[44] For a comprehensive treatment of the principle of catholicity, see Avery Dulles, *The Catholicity of the Church* (Oxford: Clarendon, 1985). See also Walter Principe, "Catholicity: Threat or Help to Identity?" in *Identity Issues and World Religions* (Bedford Park, Australia: Australian Association for the Study of Religions, 1986), 224–33.

[45] See John Meier, *Antioch and Rome: New Testament Cradles of Catholic Christianity* (New York: Paulist, 1983), 74–75.

[46] Robert Eno, "Consensus and Doctrine: Three Ancient Views," *Eglise et Théologie* 9 (1978): 480.

[47] "*Securus judicat orbis terrarum bonos non esse, qui se dissident ab orbe terrarum*" (It is not good that there be dissent from the secure judgment of the entire world) (*Contra Epist. Parmeniani* III.4.24). Eno argues that by these words, "Augustine emphasizes the *current* consensus of the world episcopate and the Catholic Church as a whole. . . . Unlike the Donatists, the Catholics of Africa were in unity, peace and communion with the rest of the universal church, the church of Rome, the churches of Asia Minor and Jerusalem" (emphasis added). Thus, Augustine's sense of

communion. While he did not disregard the ancient consensus of faith, nor the need for a firm assertion of episcopal authority in guaranteeing a common confession, he understood church councils as "a concrete manifestation of the consensus of the Church at a given moment in its life."[48] He therefore emphasized catholicity as the communion of faith, unity achieved at a particular point in the church's history through general consensus among the particular churches about faith's central content.

These two variant interpretations, one calling for a uniformitarian catholicity based on centrally regulated ecclesial uniformity of teaching and practice, the other for a substantial unity of faith through a consensus among the local churches concerning the meaning of revealed truth, would establish the twofold pattern for understanding the catholicity of the church throughout its history. The former would emphasize the role of a central teaching and jurisdictional authority, the latter the underlying patterns of the life of faith found among the baptized throughout the world. In both, however, dogmatic teaching would function as an instrument of unity, drawing disparate points of view into a union of faith, one through an emphasis on teaching authority, the other through an emphasis on the consensus of the faithful about the content of faith. And as the need for dogmatic teaching became more acute, so too did its relation to the meaning of the church's catholicity become more crucial.

In our time, the question of what constitutes a catholic unity is posed amidst the phenomenon of "inculturation"—the adaption of the faith to various cultures, and the appropriation by diverse cultures of specific traditions and theologies. As Alwyd Shorter, an expert on inculturation, explains:

> It never happens that meanings alone are communicated from one culture to another. On the contrary, the reciprocal borrowing of cul-

---

catholicity rests as much on contemporary consensus about doctrine, mediated through the episcopacy, as on ancient understandings of faith. "Consensus and Doctrine: Three Ancient Views," 476–79. Eno argues that Augustine came to see a stronger role for the primacy of the pope in his dealings with the Pelagians. See *Rise of the Papacy*, 70–74. See also Newman's discussion of Augustine's maxim in *Apologia pro vita sua*, ed. David J. DeLaura (New York: Norton, 1968), 98.

[48] Eno, "Consensus and Doctrine: Three Ancient Views," 477.

tural elements also takes place. But this raises the further problem of pluralism of meaning. . . . The transfer of religious meaning from one symbol-system to another cannot occur without dramatic modifications of symbolic patterns on one side or the other.[49]

Inculturation thus implies that the catholicity of the faith is marked by a certain pluriformity of faith expressions in the particular churches of specific cultures or within cultures: liturgical variations, characteristic practical and ethical emphases, and distinctive theological traditions.[50] From the point of view of inculturation, the meaning of catholicity leans toward the Augustinian side, searching for a universal consensus about the core of faith but allowing more and more for particular articulations and expressions of it.

This is not to say, of course, that there are not some who would subscribe to a uniformity of faith throughout the world achieved through a single interpretation and articulation of teaching and practice. But with the recognition of the fact of inculturation, the catholicity of the church suggests not an abstract universal, lending itself to uniformity, "but a *concrete* universal, one not in spite of but precisely in and because of the variety of the local churches."[51] The sheer diversity of the inculturations of faith raises in new and inescapable ways the perennial problem for the church: how to maintain both diversity and unity within a faith tradition that is

[49] Alwyd Shorter, *Revelation and Its Interpretation* (London: Geoffrey Chapman, 1983), 249. Inculturation is not a wholly new phenomenon. Much of the history of the church's growth can be read through the filter of inculturation. See, for example, the controversy concerning the efforts of Cyril and Methodius to adapt the faith to the language and customs of the Slavonic peoples in Joseph P. Fitzpatrick, *One Church, Many Cultures: The Challenge of Diversity* (Kansas City, Mo.: Sheed & Ward, 1987), 54–61. For a situating of catholicity within the context of inculturation, see Walter Principe, "Catholicity, Inculturation and Liberation Theology: Do They Mix?" *Franciscan Studies* 47 (1987): 24–43.

[50] For a thoroughgoing discussion of the issues involved in relating theologies arising from inculturation (local theologies) to the older traditions, see Robert Schreiter, *Constructing Local Theologies* (Maryknoll, N.Y.: Orbis, 1986).

[51] See Joseph A. Komonchak, "The Local Realization of the Church," in *The Reception of Vatican II*, ed. Giuseppe Alberigo, Jean-Pierre Jossua, and Joseph A. Komonchak (Washington, D.C.: Catholic University of America, 1987), 78.

flexible enough to admit of various interpretations of its content. "The crucial question presented by biblical, doctrinal, liturgical, and spiritual pluralism is whether we find a common central focus in all of the supposedly authentic ways of Christian witness past and present."[52] It is in the midst of this pluralism that we ask whether and how dogma can function today as an instrument of catholic unity within the church.

A Communion of Local Churches

This question is rendered all the more acute given the Second Vatican Council's opening up of the notion of "local" church and local church ecclesiology. In several council documents, one finds acknowledgment of the fact that the Catholic Church is realized within the local churches, and that each of the local churches is an authentic instance of the one church catholic. The *locus classicus* of this opening is found in *Lumen gentium (The Dogmatic Constitution on the Church in the Modern World)*, which teaches that "the whole mystical body . . . is also a body of churches."[53] *Lumen gentium* elaborates:

> This church of Christ is truly present in all the lawful congregations [*congregationibus localibus*] of the faithful which, united to their shepherds, are themselves called churches in the New Testament. For in their own locality [*loco suo*], these are the new people called by God in the holy Spirit and with full conviction (see 1 Th 1.5). . . . In these communities, although frequently small and poor, or dispersed, Christ is present by whose power the one, holy catholic and apostolic church is gathered together.[54]

An earlier passage of *Lumen gentium* extends the notion of local church from its application to the various sister churches of the East to bishops' conferences within the Roman Catholic Church itself:

> By divine providence it has come about that various churches, founded in various places by the apostles and by their successors, have in the course of time become joined together into several

[52] Jeanrond, *Theological Hermeneutics*, 176.

[53] *Lumen gentium*, 23, in *Decrees of the Ecumenical Councils*, 2:867 (DS 4147).

[54] *Lumen gentium*, 26, in *Decrees of the Ecumenical Councils*, 2:870 (DS 4151).

groups, organically united, which, while maintaining the unity of faith and the unique divine constitution of the universal church, enjoy their own discipline, their own liturgical usage and their own theological and spiritual patrimony. Among these there are some, especially the ancient patriarchal churches, like matrices of the faith, which have given birth to others as daughters; and right down to our own times they are more closely bound to these churches by the bond of charity in sacramental life and in mutual respect for rights and duties. This variety of local churches, in harmony among themselves, demonstrates with greater clarity the catholicity of the undivided church. In a similar way episcopal conferences can today make a manifold and fruitful contribution to the concrete application of the spirit of collegiality.[55]

Even more clearly, *Ad gentes* (*Decree on the Missionary Activity of the Church*) addresses the role of local churches as incarnations of the one catholic faith. The language anticipates the theologies of inculturation that would appear after the council:

Indeed, as with the economy of the incarnation, the young churches, rooted in Christ and built on the foundation of the apostles, take over, in a marvelous exchange, all the riches of the nations which have been given to Christ as an inheritance [see Ps 2:8]. From the customs and traditions of their own peoples, from their wisdom and learning, from their arts and sciences, these churches borrow everything which can contribute to praising the glory of the creator, to making manifest the grace of the savior and to the due regulation of Christian life. . . . Finally, the particular young churches, enriched by their own traditions, will have their due place in the community of

---

[55] *Lumen gentium*, 23, in *Decrees of the Ecumenical Councils* 2:868 (DS 4147). Karl Rahner writes of this passage: "It is to be noted that though only formulated as a historical observation, the first sentence of the section involves an important principle, since the historical findings are regarded as marking a special divine providence. It affects particularly the Latin or Western branch of the Catholic Church because this has in fact been practically identified with the Church as a whole. Major Churches with their own discipline, their own liturgy and their own spiritual and theological heritage could also be formed in the future, by 'divine providence', say in Africa, Asia or South America." *Commentary on the Documents of Vatican II*, vol. 1; ed. Herbert Vorgrimler (New York: Herder and Herder, 1969), 207.

[56] *Ad gentes,* 50, in *Decrees of the Ecumenical Councils*, 2:1030–31.

the church, while the primacy of the see of Peter, which presides over this universal assembly of charity, remains fully respected.[56]

The council thus affirms that the universal church in fact exists precisely in and through the local churches, which are constituted of people who live in particular times, places, cultures, and traditions. The Catholic Church is therefore understood here not according to a vertical model alone, as of headquarters to branch offices, but also horizontally, potentially as a *communio* of a variety of local churches, each of which, singularly and in communion with the others, instantiates the universality of the church's faith and the oneness of the church itself.[57] Catholicity is not the sum of the parts of all the local churches together, but the realization of the catholicity of faith in each local church, each of which is thereby also brought into communion with the others. Hence, each local church should be able to recognize in the other the one Catholic faith in Jesus Christ, the gospel of salvation, and the liturgical and evangelical works of charity that make that faith real in the lives of Christians. This notion of local church, taught by the council, renders the issue of dogma's unifying function both challenging and inescapable. It is not merely a theoretical question, but one whose implications finally go to the core of our understanding of the nature of the church.[58]

[57] See Joseph A. Komonchak, "The Church Universal as the Communion of Local Churches," in *Where Does the Church Stand?* ed. Giuseppe Alberigo and Gustavo Gutierrez (New York: Seabury, 1981), 30–35. See also Richard P. McBrien, "The Ecclesiology of the Local Church," *Thought* 66 (1991): 359–67, who writes: "Although the relationship between the universal and local expressions of the Body of Christ is not made precise in the New Testament, it is clear that we do not have a Corinthian division of the church, for example, but 'the church of God which is in Corinth' (1 Cor. 1.2). On the other hand, the church is a living, integrated organism: 'the fullness of him who fills the universe in all its parts' (Eph 1.23)." The council does not itself actually teach a *communio* ecclesiology; the various teachings of the council appear to have been received within an ecclesial context where this reading became prevalent. See Komonchak, "Local Realization of the Church," 77.

[58] Schreiter notes: "Local theology is certainly not anything new to Christianity. But a direct awareness and pursuit of it is relatively recent for most Christian churches. For Roman Catholics, the stress on universality has been such that it makes it difficult to think about how locality and universality are to be related." *Constructing Local Theologies*, 37.

Some argue that not only is ecclesial pluralism not in(
with the unity of Catholic truth, but that a pluralism of faith e₍ₓₚ₎
sions is essential to the unity of Catholic faith in the post-conciliar
period.[59] But pluralism is of value to the degree that it serves the
cause of unity in faith through the authenticity of the life of the
faith in the local churches. Cultural pluralism is the context within
which ecclesial pluralism takes root; the local churches mirror the
cultures in which they live. Yet the pluralism of faith interpretations
and expressions that emerge from a culturally pluralistic situation
must be judged by some normative (and one would hope, unifying)
standard. Otherwise, the church risks chaos.

Dogma as an Instrument of Consensus

It is in the positing of a normative standard, in particular a standard
presented by a teaching authority, that tension emerges. Dogmatic
teaching in particular often seems to function not as an instrument
of the mediation of faith to culture or of culture to faith, but as a
stumbling block to understanding, even to people within the
church itself. Indeed, with certain questions such as birth control
and women's ordination, church teaching itself has become the
issue within a culturally and ecclesially pluralistic situation. Pluralism within the church thus risks becoming a title that merely digni-
fies "the ultimacy of disagreement."[60] Yet agreeing to disagree, or
settling for some secular ideal of "civility," is not the unity of faith
the church has sought since its inception. Nor will the sometimes
intractable problems raised by pluralism simply disappear by the
apodictic imposition of a rule or forced closure of dialogue. Plu-

---

[59] See, e.g., Godehard Lindgens, "Pluralismus und Christentum: Studie
zur katholischen Theorie über das Verhältnis von Pluralismus und
Wahrheit," *Freiburger Zeitschrift für Philosophie und Theologie* 29 (1982):
465–87. In this article, the author takes issue with Oswald Nell-Breuning,
who held that normative pluralism was not the position of the Second Vatican Council. Lindgens argues that authentic pluralism is possible within
the church, as long as the truth of faith is conceived not solely as an
abstract construct but rather as a practical, concrete, lived, and experienced truth.

[60] See Alasdair MacIntyre, *After Virtue*, 2d ed. (Notre Dame, Ind.: University of Notre Dame Press, 1984), 32.

ralism arises from and reflects human reality. It is in the midst of this reality that dogma must function as an instrument of unity.

As noted above, Augustine faced an analogous problem in religiously polymorphous Africa. There he was centrally involved in the struggle to arrive at a normative articulation of Christian faith amidst a pluralism of theological interpretations. Unity within pluralism could be reached, he argued, through the consensus of the faithful about the content of faith, what the entire Christian world judges to be true through years of practice and confession of faith.[61] This consensus is the realization of unity, not only the means to it. Such consensus rests on the *sensus fidei* (sense of faith) held by all baptized persons who live their faith and constitute the church of a particular time and place. This "sense of the faith" held by all the faithful, has become a recurring theme in theological reflection since the Second Vatican Council. The council elaborated on this theme in *Lumen gentium*:

> The universal body of the faithful who have received the anointing of the holy one, cannot be mistaken in belief. It displays this particular quality through a supernatural sense of the faith in the whole people when "from the bishops to the last of the faithful laity" (cf. Augustine, *De Praed. Sanct., PL* 44:980), it expresses the consent of all in matters of faith and morals. Through this sense of faith which is aroused and sustained by the Spirit of truth, the people of God, under the guidance of the sacred magisterium to which it is faithfully obedient, receives no longer the words of human beings but truly the word of God; it adheres indefectibly to "the faith which was once for all delivered to the saints" (Jude 3); it penetrates more deeply into that same faith through right judgment and applies it more fully to life.[62]

The council thus acknowledges and embraces a tenet long held within the tradition of the church, that the faith is received and

---

[61] For a discussion of this idea, see Principe, "Catholicity: A Threat or Help to Identity?" 225–26.

[62] *Lumen gentium*, 12, in *Decrees of the Ecumenical Councils*, 2:858 (DS 4130). Another key text is *Dei verbum* [8]. For a thorough discussion of both these passages, see Sullivan, *Magisterium*, 17–21. For a discussion of the use of *sensus fidei* by the Second Vatican Council, see Zoltán Alszeghy, "The 'Sensus Fidei' and the Development of Dogma," in *Vatican II: Assessment and Perspectives*, vol. 1, ed. René Latourelle (New York: Paulist, 1988), 138–56.

transmitted not solely through the teaching authorities, bu
through the life of faith of all the faithful, the *sensus fidelium* (sense
of faith of the faithful).[63] This universal sense of faith, or concor-
dance in matters of faith, is captured by another term, the *consensus
fidelium* (the consensus or agreement of the faithful), which played
a significant role in Newman's effort to articulate the nature and
function of dogma within the church.

There are, then, three terms operating here: *sensus fidei, sensus
fidelium,* and *consensus fidelium.* These require some further elaboration. Herbert Vorgrimler describes the *sensus fidei* as a knowledge
of faith granted to those who possess faith, the *sensus fidelium* as the
collective faith consciousness of the faithful, and the *consensus
fidelium* as the "agreement which arises among believers as a result
of the sense of faith with regard to particular items of faith."[64] Francis Sullivan adds that "the term *consensus fidelium* (agreement of the
faithful) adds the element of universal agreement to the notion of
sensus fidelium. It refers to the situation in which, on a particular
issue of faith, the whole body of the faithful, 'from the bishops
down to the last member of the laity', share the same belief."[65]
Congar holds that the term *sensus fidei* refers to a certain instinct for
the content and living of faith to be found in individual believers
and in the church as a whole, the fruit of ecclesial communion.
Congar would take both views into account in defining the *sensus
fidei,* the personal and the ecclesial. Congar also notes the tendency
among modern theologians to equate the sense of faith with "consciousness" (*conscience*) in the psychological sense of intuition or a
more or less clear sense of its own state or of its own acts. Against
this, he argues that we must not forget that that of which the church
is conscious is something that is given to it, a gift received. The
church's self-consciousness is a consciousness of a living memory of

[63] Mahoney remarks that in recent years there has been a "recovered
view of the whole Church as transcending the nineteenth-century division
into teaching and learning Church" and that the "teaching" authority of
the church rests not only in the magisterium and theologians but also in
the faithful as a whole, who are in moral communication with one
another. See *Making of Moral Theology,* 161, 223.

[64] Herbert Vorgrimler, "From *Sensus Fidei* to *Consensus Fidelium,*" in *The
Authority of the Believers,* ed. Johannes-Baptist Metz and Edward Schillebeeckx (Edinburgh: T. & T. Clark, 1985), 3

[65] Sullivan, *Magisterium,* 23.

that which the church has received. Thus, the *sensus fidei* is not the sum total of many individual instances of faith consciousness, but the fruit of the "communion" of faith, a communion of sanctity in which all share by virtue of baptism. The *consensus fidelium* should be understood in a similar sense.[66]

In light of this communion model of faith in the church, the problem that dogma faces is how it can function as an instrument of ecclesial unity. Experience has shown how doubtful it is that a symbolic expression of faith, even an authoritative teaching of the magisterium, can guarantee consensus. The pluriformity of the church, made evident in divergent inculturations of the faith and in local theologies, militates against the ability of dogma to unify the church. Add to this the narrowing of the theme of dogma to authoritative propositions alone and the problem looms substantial. Dogma can serve as an instrument of unity only if it can both speak to and be appropriated by peoples of very specific times and places. This calls for approaches to dogma in which, without losing its normative authority as church teaching, it also serves as the initiator of dialogue about the meaning of faith and its critical transmission. In the dialogue it initiates, and in which peoples of the various cultures of the churches participate, a universal consensus of faith could emerge, a catholic unity. The contemporary problem with dogma thus becomes part of the larger perennial problem of the transmission of tradition through the unfolding history of faith. How, then, do we approach dogma in order to arrive at such an understanding of its function in the life of the church?

APPROACHING DOGMA ANEW

This brief survey of the history of dogma as a concept, together with the contemporary context of ecclesial pluralism within which dogma must be understood, poses three challenges as we try to recover a unifying function for dogma in the church.

First, it is important to remember that dogma is in the first instance a theme of the life of faith, not only propositional teaching. This means that a fresh approach to dogma must include its original rich texture, not only as a propositional expression of the

[66] Congar, *La Tradition et les traditions*, vol. 2, *Essai théologique*, 83–86.

church's teaching of faith but also as the confession of faith expressed in liturgical, disciplinary, and theological traditions.

Second, dogma is a function of the catholicity of the church, where the mark of catholicity is understood (in the conciliar sense) as a *communio*. While dogma is therefore properly viewed in relation to the teaching function of the church, it must also be viewed in relation to the critical reception and appropriation of that teaching by the people of the local churches through their particular faith traditions. Consensus is reached through a range of liturgical, disciplinary, and theological traditions.

Third, because dogma is the historically conditioned teaching and confession of faith, it is a constitutive part of the faith tradition, and does not reign in abstraction from it. It continually discloses the content of faith in new ways even as it is appropriated in the life of faith lived in history.

The first of these challenges requires that we work toward an understanding of dogma that includes but is not limited to the propositional matter that the church teaches, but embraces also how the church confesses its faith—the whole of the church's faith expression—in and through (1) liturgical practices (e.g., a multiplicity of and variation among rites), (2) the disciplines of particular churches (e.g., priestly marriage in some rites, celibacy in others), and (3) even particular theological approaches to understanding the creedal content of faith, a content that is universally accepted (e.g., a Latin American theology of liberation or a North American feminist theology). Such a view of dogma would be more in keeping with its original usage, before the earliest councils and especially before its delimitation to authoritative teaching of the church, particularly teachings of the Roman magisterium.

The second challenge is to reimagine the church, not simply on the bi-level model of *ecclesia docens* (church teaching) and *ecclesia discens* (church taught) but as a communion of learners and teachers who actualize the faith catholic in the various local churches. Giuseppe Alberigo envisions such a church as "circular and intertwined, . . . in which every believer and every community is simultaneously subject and object."[67] While primatial and episcopal church teaching enjoys a pride of place in the hierarchy of dogmatic

[67] Giuseppe Alberigo, "The Christian Situation after Vatican II," in *The Reception of Vatican II*, 6.

ons as we currently understand dogma, such teaching does
..self guarantee catholic unity. That unity depends in part
also on the degree to which the teachers themselves listen to and
appropriate what is being taught, and the degree to which the
entire church freely engages in a process of appropriation that leads
to ecclesial faith consensus.

The third challenge is to arrive at an understanding of dogma
that will allow for ongoing adaptation to reality and a sense of hope
within the Christian community.[68] Here we must see dogma as a
constitutive part of the tradition of faith itself, and we must understand at least some dogmatic change (propositional, liturgical, disciplinary, theological) as a part of the process whereby the truth of
the faith tradition is transmitted and appropriated in specific times
and places, and by the church at large.

A book of this size cannot possibly treat the full range of these
challenges exhaustively. The first would require a massive historical
treatment of dogma and would require that we examine the history
of the faith tradition itself and its various dogmatic expressions.
This is properly an exercise in historical theology or the history of
ideas. Such a history can only be presupposed and at times referred
to here. The second thrusts us into the realm of ecclesiology, the
exercise of primacy and episcopacy, and the specific nature and
function of the magisterium of the church, especially in relation to
the laity. While this is an indispensable part of the overall picture,
it too lies beyond the scope of this more limited project, except
insofar as I turn to the role that the faithful play in expressing the
life of faith, and advert to the necessity of an authoritative episcopal and primatial magisterium within the life of the church. I will
therefore prescind from lengthy ecclesiological excursions or specific recommendations about how the magisterium ought to teach,
or the shape that the magisterium might play in the future. This is
not an essay in ecclesiology.

The third challenge drives to the heart of the retrieval of
dogma's unifying function: how dogma can serve as an instrument

---

[68] "In concrete terms this involves the question of how the church can
continue to transmit its binding teaching of the faith in such a way as to
allow hope for the present and the future to emerge from the retrieval of
tradition." International Theological Commission, "On the Interpretation
of Dogmas," 1–14.

of unity when the truth of faith is transmitted and appropriated by the various local instantiations of the one church in a variety of dogmatic expressions (propositional, liturgical, disciplinary, and theological). While church teaching or universal church practices often represent the promise of catholic unity, that unity finally rests in the appropriation of the faith tradition in specific times and places by the people of the various local churches. Yet the reality of pluralism means that there will be a multiplicity of perspectives and dogmatic expressions about the single unifying content of the faith tradition that has always been and always will be proposed by the magisterium. The unity of faith, catholicity, rests not simply on uniform interpretation of church teaching but, more fundamentally, on the consensus of faith that arises from the appropriation of it by the faithful of actual local churches, an appropriation in turn expressed through a variety of other dogmatic symbols—liturgical, disciplinary, and theological—generated within local church traditions. This approach plays off both of the first two challenges—a broader understanding of dogma than is often assumed and a specific concern for the role of the faithful in arriving at an articulation of the *consensus fidelium.*

Focusing on this third challenge raises three further concerns about how dogma functions. First, if dogma is to be seen as more than propositional matter alone, and also as a confession of faith that mediates the truth of the faith tradition to the changing and pluralistic historical and cultural conditions of the people of the church, then it must be understood as faithfully embodying or expressing the selfsame substantial truth of faith to cultures even as dogma itself undergoes change in its form. This raises the classic question of how dogmatic change and the unchanging nature of revealed truth can be reconciled with each other, a question that runs as a subtheme in the pages that follow. But, second, if the church is to be understood partly as a community of faith consensus, a community of learners and teachers, then some accounting must also be made for the role that the "mind" or faith consciousness of the church plays in the formulation, transmission, and appropriation of dogmatic symbols, and how contemporary horizons of faith meet the ancient faith tradition symbolized in dogmas. And, third, if dogma as teaching is to function as an instrument of unity, it must do this in such a way as to be received and interpreted by the people of the church who live within particular cultures and with specific horizons of understanding, allowing for some perspectival differences in understanding the truth expressed by dogma. Dogma may then function in such a way as to engender ongoing consensus within the world church about the truth and implications of faith in Jesus Christ as the definitive revelation of God.

Each of these functions of dogma—faithful expression of the selfsame truth of revelation, mediation of the faith to a catholic church constituted of local churches, and ongoing local interpretation and application—is indispensable to the successful functioning of dogma as an instrument of unity. When dogma functions as a constitutive and thematic part of a living tradition, then it also offers hope for a tradition that is in living relation to the world in which it is rooted. It was such a living tradition that John Henry Newman sought as he pondered his conversion to Roman Catholicism, and it is to his original opening up of the question of dogma that we now turn: dogma as "idea" of revelation.

CHAPTER 2

Dogma as "Idea" of Revelation

The facts of Revealed Religion, though in their substance unaltered, present a less compact and orderly front to the attacks of its enemies now than formerly, and allow of the introduction of new inquiries and theories concerning its sources and its rise. . . . The assailants of dogmatic truth have got the start of its adherents of whatever Creed. . . . An argument is needed, unless Christianity is to abandon the province of argument.

—John Henry Newman[1]

John Henry Newman was one of those seminal thinkers to whom generations of scholars have turned again and again, partly because of his careful and ingenious reading of ancient Christian sources. Born a member of the evangelical Anglican Church (Church of England), Newman later became an Anglican priest. But he found both the evangelical forms of Christianity and the newer "liberal" theologies too dismissive of Christian tradition. As a leader of the "Oxford Movement" between 1833 and 1845, he struggled with the role that dogma should play in the church. Yet it would be a clear case of anachronism to attribute to Newman an explicit interest in the specific question we are dealing with in this book, the unifying function of dogma. Newman's famous excur-

---

[1] *An Essay on the Development of Christian Doctrine,* 1878 rev. ed., ed. Charles Harrold (London: Longmans, 1949), 29–30. Throughout this chapter we will use this 1878 edition, Newman's own revision of his original 1845 work.

35

suses on doctrine, in both the Oxford University Sermons[2] and in the *Essay on the Development of Doctrine,* were composed during his Anglican period when he was in the process of trying to justify (mostly to himself) the plausibility of the authentic development of Roman Catholicism from primitive Christianity, the church of the fathers.

Newman's involvement in the Oxford Movement between 1833 and 1845 provided the theological background and personal impetus for his preoccupation with dogma. In collaboration with his Oxford colleagues John Keble, R. Hurrell Froude, and others, Newman felt driven to be able to establish the nature and authority of the Church of England not on the state but on the bedrock of apostolic succession, on an authority deriving from Jesus and the apostles. This had become more than an academic question. In 1833 Parliament had disestablished—that is, dissolved—several Irish bishoprics (dioceses) of the Church of England. Keble, a Fellow of Oriel College, saw this as evidence that the Church of England had abandoned its apostolic foundation and had become, in practice, a tool of the state. He also saw in this event the triumph of the so-called liberal elements within the Church of England who were willing to forsake doctrinal orthodoxy for political expediency. His famous Assize Sermon, the "National Apostasy," is commonly viewed as the initial salvo fired by the Oxford party against the liberals.[3] Keble's words galvanized a number of Oxford Anglicans, including Newman, to take up the cause of apostolic Christianity.

> [Keble could not see] how any person can devote himself too entirely to the cause of the Apostolical Church in these realms. There may be, as far as he knows, but a very few to sympathize with him. He

[2] For the Oxford University Sermons, see *Newman's University Sermons: Fifteen Sermons Preached before the University of Oxford 1826–43 by John Henry Newman* (London: S.P.C.K., 1970). This is a reprint of the 1871 (3d) edition.

[3] In 1864 Newman himself said of the occasion of Keble's sermon: "I have ever considered and kept the day, as the start of the religious movement of 1833." *Apologia pro vita sua,* 152. For a discussion by Newman of the multivalent senses of the term "liberal" in his own day, see "Note A: Liberalism" in the *Apologia.* For a discussion of liberalism and its theological implications, see John R. Quinn, "Cardinal Newman: A Study in Integrity," *Origins* 20/35 (February 7, 1991): 579–84.

may have to wait long, and very likely pass out of this world before he sees any abatement of the triumph of disorder and irreligion. But, if he be consistent, he possesses, to the utmost, the personal consolation of a good Christian: and as a true Churchman, he has that encouragement, which no other cause in the world can impart in the same degree:—he is calmly, soberly, demonstrably, sure, that sooner or later, his will be the winning side, and that the victory will be complete, universal, eternal.[4]

Newman, too, felt strongly that the Anglican Church had to confront "irreverence towards Antiquity, the unscrupulous and wanton violation of the commands and usages of our forefathers" and "the growing indifference to the Catholic Creed."[5] He, too, found himself at odds with the liberals, who for him embodied the "anti-dogmatic principle and its developments."[6] As an Anglican, Newman was troubled that he would not have to argue before Roman Catholics in favor of such givens as apostolic succession or the sacrificial theology of eucharist. But it is also true that at least until 1840, Newman remained very firmly opposed to the apparent doctrinal innovations of the Roman Church. In some of his writings, he was to link both the pope and the Roman Church with the anti-Christ.[7] And much of his intellectual effort between 1833 and 1840 was to be devoted to the search for a middle course, the *Via Media*, between Protestantism and Catholicism, which Anglicanism could claim as its own.

His purpose was therefore in many ways very uniquely personal; he was concerned about the authenticity of his faith. Still, the background to his investigations was the "liberalism" of the nineteenth-century Anglican Church—a rationalistic bent of mind suspicious of revealed truth and the continuing validity of the classical expressions of Christian faith. Liberalism led to one thing only: atheism,

[4] John Keble, "National Apostasy, Considered in a Sermon Preached in St. Mary's Oxford before His Majesty's Judges of Assize on Sunday, July 14th, 1833," in *Keble's Assize Sermon* (London: Mowbray, 1931), 23–24.

[5] Newman, "Sermon IX: Wilfulness, the Sin of Saul," in *Newman's University Sermons*, 174.

[6] Newman, *Apologia pro vita sua*, 163.

[7] Ibid., 223–24. Even in 1841 he was to charge that the Church of Rome in England lacked any marks of sanctity, although the grounds of his Anglican identity were growing ever more unstable.

"simple unbelief in matters of religion."[8] It was this frame of mind that led to the fragmentation of the Christian church and the development of inauthentic forms of Christianity. Newman was thus ardently concerned about how dogma could function in such a way as to meet the challenges posed by the crisis of liberalism. How could he be sure that he was not proposing a view of Christianity every bit as flimsy as liberalism was in its own way? His search would take him back to the French coastal island of Lerins, and to the fifth century.

THE LEGACY OF VINCENT OF LERINS

In taking on liberalism, Newman was up against a problem that had been expressed fifteen centuries earlier by the monk and theologian Vincent of Lerins: the relationship between the immutable revealed truth that dogmatic teachings express and the mutability of the formulas used to express it. The traditional position of the church was that truth, if revealed, cannot change. Yet, Newman argued, the appearance of dogmas in the history of the church is a clear instance of linguistic change. If language changes, then does the truth expressed in that language suffer some sort of mutation as well?[9] If it does, then we are left with a relativism that would prove congenial to the liberal Anglican mind but which would only undermine the integrity of the catholic faith.

In his influential *Commonitorium* (434), Vincent asked whether apparent progress (*profectus*) in the expression of revealed truth signified an essential change in the truth itself.[10] His answer, summa-

[8] See Newman, *Apologia pro vita sua*, 160.

[9] In the *Essay* and in the University Sermons, Newman is focusing on dogma as propositional matter, that is, as "doctrine." But, as we shall see, Newman expands his field of data, so that dogma includes various other elements of the church's confession of faith, not only propositions of belief and teaching.

[10] Although little known during the Middle Ages, the post-Reformation return to ancient sources of faith along with the need to update Catholicism saw a burgeoning of interest in the *Commonitorium*: 35 editions and 22 translations in the sixteenth century, 23 editions and 12 translations in the seventeenth, 12 editions and 12 translations in the eighteenth, and 15 editions and 21 translations in the nineteenth. See G. Bardy, "Vincent of

rized in what became called the "Vincentian Canon," was a resounding no. The truth of Catholic faith was *quod ubique, quod semper, quod ab omnibus creditum est*:

> In the Catholic Church itself, every care should be taken to hold fast to what has been believed everywhere, always and by all. This is truly and properly "Catholic," as indicated by the force and etymology of the name itself, which comprises everything truly universal. This general rule will be truly applied if we follow the principles of universality, antiquity, and consent. We do so in regard to universality if we confess that faith alone to be true which the entire Church confesses all over the world. [We do so] in regard to antiquity if we in no way deviate from those interpretations which our ancestors and fathers have manifestly proclaimed [*celebrasse manifestum est*] as inviolable. [We do so] in regard to consent if, in this very antiquity, we adopt the definitions and propositions of all, or almost all, the bishops and doctors.[11]

That which is properly "catholic" states what has been held everywhere in the world (geographic universality), from as far back as historical memory will allow (antiquity), and by all adherents to the faith, as represented in the consistency of the teachings of bishops and theologians (consent). Universality, antiquity, and consent are therefore guarantees that a given dogma is a bona fide expression of revealed truth; if the dogma is a new formulation not found in scripture (e.g., the Chalcedonian Definition of the two natures, human and divine, united in the person of Christ), then this is an example of growth in the forms of faith (*profectus religionis*); but such growth cannot contradict the principles of universality, antiquity, and consent.[12] The truth of faith is immutable, and change in the dogmatic formulation of the truth of faith can be granted only if this change does not imply a substantial change in the truth itself.

Lérins," *Dictionnaire de théologie catholique*, 15:3046. See also Kasper, *Dogma unter dem Wort Gottes*, 34–35.

[11] Vincent of Lerins, *Commonitorium*, chapter 2, as in "The Commonitories," in *The Fathers of the Church: A New Translation*, trans. Rudolph E. Morris (New York, N.Y.: Fathers of the Church, Inc., 1949), 270–71. See Migne, *Patrologiae cursus completus, Series Latina [PL]*, ed. J. P. Migne (Paris, 1846), 50:640.

[12] Vincent of Lerins, *Commonitorium*, chapter 23, 308; *PL* 5:667–68.

But much would hinge on exactly how this "Vincentian Canon" would be interpreted, especially its notion of a *profectus religionis*.

Interpreting "Profectus Religionis"

Since dogmatic formulations are themselves subject to the criteria of universality, antiquity, and consent, *profectus religionis* could be rendered a rather recondite concept. As Pelikan has noted, the universality and unanimous consent accorded revealed truth (the *quod ubique* and *quod ab omnibus*) have to rest ultimately on the fact that the one and same truth has been held from the most ancient of times (*quod semper*). "The true doctrine was the most ancient. Therefore, it was also the most contemporary, for it went on being confessed from generation to generation, all of whom were embraced in the 'ever.'"[13]

If Vincent were to be interpreted rigidly, change in the propositional expression of revealed truth would seem to be limited at best to the drawing of logical inferences from the propositions of old, lest the immutability of the revealed truth itself be jeopardized. No authentic change in dogma could be accounted for as this would necessarily imply a change in revealed truth. In fact, this kind of position influenced several Catholic theologians of the nineteenth century, led by J. B. Franzelin at the First Vatican Council.[14] Dogmatic development was so severely suspect as to be limited to exercises in logical deduction. This situation resulted in part because the *quod semper* seemed logically to be the most powerful element in the Vincentian Canon.

But the Vincentian Canon could also be read more flexibly. In the "second rule" of chapter 23 of the *Commonitorium*, a *profectus religionis* is possible because the truth held by the church as a whole, by its individual members in communion with one another, remains itself even as it is only gradually known more deeply. In a

[13] Pelikan, *Historical Theology*, 5–6.

[14] Thomas J. Guarino, "Vincent of Lerins and the Hermeneutical Question," *Gregorianum* 75 (1994): 491–523. Guarino also argues that some nineteenth-century theologians, particularly of the Tübingen school (J. A. Möhler and J. E. Kuhn), made use of Vincent to support the plausibility of historical development of tradition.

passage that was to inspire Newman and others, Vincent himself opened the door to a less restrictive understanding and compared the *profectus religionis* to the growth of a child into an adult. Although growth occurs, there is no change in the child's essential identity:

> There remains one and the same nature and one and the same person. . . . In the same way the dogma of the Christian religion ought to follow these laws of progress, so that it may be consolidated in the course of years, developed in the sequence of time, and sublimated by age—yet remain incorrupt and unimpaired, complete and perfect in all the proportions of its parts and in all of its essentials . . . so that it does not allow any change, or any loss of its specific character, or any variation of its inherent form.[15]

This passage cleared the way for a theory of dogmatic development that in effect ties the immutability of revealed truth to the principle of substantial self-identity through linguistic change, an insight on which Newman would capitalize. But Vincent's *profectus* "does not allow any change" in the Christian faith "or any loss of its specific character, or any variation of its inherent form."

> To be sure, there has to be progress [*profectus*], even exceedingly great progress. . . . But it must be progress in the proper sense of the word, and not a change [*permutatio*] in faith. Progress means that each thing grows within itself, whereas change implies that one thing is transformed into another. Hence, it must be that understanding, knowledge, and wisdom grow and advance mightily and strongly in individuals as well as in the community, in a single person as well as in the Church as a whole, and this gradually according to age and history. But they must progress within their own limits, that is, in accordance with the same kind of dogma, frame of mind, and intellectual approach.[16]

Profectus is thus distinguished from *permutatio*, growth from transformation, development from substantial change.[17]

---

[15] Vincent of Lerins, *Commonitorium*, chapter 23, 109–10; *PL* 5:667–68.
[16] Ibid.
[17] Guarino argues that this "second rule" of chapter 23 of the *Commonitorium* "disallows any excessive antiquarianism and indicates that Vincent did not believe that his concern for the three canonical criteria . . . mili-

The Vincentian Canon through the Centuries

The Vincentian Canon was not universally viewed as an absolute obstacle to the notion of some sort of adjustment of dogma to changing circumstances. Thomas Aquinas took such a position in his discussion of doctrinal growth in the *Summa theologiae*. He asked, "Whether articles of faith grow in accord with the advance of time?"[18] In this article, Thomas undertook a more open reading of the Vincentian Canon. The content of faith is substantially the same now as it was in the early church, and in post-apostolic development of doctrine what the apostles had taught was more sufficiently explicated (*sufficienter explicata*).[19] This position had to assume the distinction between a profound and at least implicit awareness in the minds of the apostles of the essential content of faith, which they possessed, and the more explicit intellectual knowledge of Christian mysteries, which they did not necessarily possess.[20] This line of thought squared with the traditional view that revelation had ended with the death of the apostles and that any suggestion of new revelation was impossible. But it also provided for an adjustment in the understanding of the truth of revelation and for a correlative adjustment in the formulation of this understanding that would constitute a change in dogmatic teaching itself.

Thomas further argued that new language is not necessarily equivalent to an addition to revelation.[21] For example, it was permissible for the fathers at Nicaea and Chalcedon to apply philosophical terms such as "hypostasis" to the divine persons, even though such terminology is not found explicitly in the scriptures nor in the earliest formulations of faith in the fathers. The new

---

tated against doctrinal progress." "Vincent of Lerins and the Hermeneutical Question," 493.

[18] *Summa theologiae*, 2-2, 1, 7.

[19] *Summa theologiae*, 2-2, 1, 7–10. See Edward Schillebeeckx, "The Development of the Apostolic Faith into the Dogma of the Church," in *Revelation and Theology*, vol. 1, trans. N. D. Smith (New York: Sheed & Ward, 1967), 59.

[20] See Schillebeeckx, *Revelation and Theology*, 1:59–60; and Lash, *Change in Focus*, 51–52.

[21] *Summa theologiae* 1, 29, 3.

terms refer to the once-given truth which has always been held by the church but which has lacked only explicit formulation.

In 1439, the Council of Florence in effect endorsed such a view by granting the validity of the creed of the Eastern churches on the spiration of the Holy Spirit from the Father and the Son, thus implicitly accepting the possibility that not all parts of the revealed truth are necessarily made explicit in single formulations.[22] Dulles holds that the Council of Florence "showed an exemplary breadth of understanding. It affirmed that the unity of the Church should be built not on particular doctrinal formulas, but rather 'on the cornerstone, Christ Jesus, who will make both one.' . . . An agreement based on mutual tolerance was reached regarding the crucial question of the procession of the Holy Spirit."[23]

A subtle but significant change occurred at the Council of Trent, where, in the shadow of the Vincentian Canon, universal assent to revealed truth was especially emphasized.[24] Such assent was thought to be evidenced not merely by adherence to doctrinal formulations uniformly throughout the world but also by adherence and consent to the church's practices (*traditiones*). The Council of Trent did not simply equate authentic Catholic truth with the most ancient formulas of faith. It broadened the content of what merited universal consent beyond propositions. Trent's use of *fides* stood in the medieval tradition. It denoted neither belief (*opinio*) nor theoretical knowledge (*scientia*) alone, but was tied to "everything that the Church universally imposes in the order of salvation: doctrine, liturgical and sacramental practice, and canon law."[25] Far from lim-

---

[22] See *Laetentur coeli* (1439), in *Decrees of the Ecumenical Councils*, 1:523–28, esp. 527 (DS 1301), which says that the Western formulation that the Holy Spirit proceeds from the Father and the Son "tends to this meaning" [*ad hanc intelligentiam tendit*]—that is, to the Eastern view of spiration.

[23] Dulles, *Survival of Dogma*, 155–75. For a less optimistic assessment of the final effect of this decree, see Pelikan, *The Christian Tradition: A History of the Development of Doctrine*, vol. 2, *The Spirit of Eastern Christendom* (Chicago: University of Chicago Press, 1974), 277.

[24] However, despite the growth in publication and translation of the *Commonitorium* during the sixteenth century, Trent did not cite Vincent. See Guarino, "Vincent of Lerins and the Hermeneutical Question," 493.

[25] Piet Fransen, "Unity and Confessional Statements: Historical and Theological Inquiry of Roman Catholic Traditional Conceptions," *Bijdra-*

iting revealed truth to propositional dogma, Trent widened the range of evidences by which the revealed truth can be known. Both the knowing of this truth in faith and subsequent dogmatic formulations are situated within a broad understanding of the church's life of faith as both teaching and confession.

It was not Trent but the three centuries of rationalism that followed it that emphasized a conceptualist approach to dogma and its exclusively propositional form.[26] The seventeenth-century French bishop Jacques-Bénigne Bossuet gave impetus to this conceptualist approach. Bossuet defended the fundamental position of the Vincentian Canon and held that the admission of any change in the ancient formulas was tantamount to the introduction of new revelation and was thus a flirtation with heresy. Bossuet invoked Tertullian, who had said that "the rule of faith is unchangeable, and is not to be reformed at all," for the church has professed to speak or teach only what it has received, and never to vary it; whereas heresy, which begins with innovation, always innovates, and by nature never ceases doing so.[27] The only proper expression of faith, even that guaranteed by the church, was that propositional articulation of faith which had always and everywhere been held as part of faith by all Catholics.

A strict reading of Vincent of Lerins, coupled with the later consolidation of the church's teaching authority into the hierarchical magisterium, was to make itself felt in the nineteenth century, well

---

gen 33 (1972): 18. See also the very balanced discussion by John Mahoney of Trent's use of *mores* in Trent's foundational document on scripture and tradition, in *Making of Moral Theology*, 120–35. Mahoney joins in a qualified agreement with Congar that this particular decree "used the noun *mores* not of moral matters but of religious practices" (ibid., 123). Thus, this decree was concerned primarily not with teaching about morals (a later interpretation) but with the relationship between the interpretation of scripture and the practices of faith.

[26] Fransen, an authority on Trent, argues: "We still suffer from the deep impact in our theological tradition of three centuries of rationalism, during which the conceptual formulation of faith was currently accepted as an evident and spontaneous function of the human mind, even in matters of faith." "Unity and Confessional Statements," 4.

[27] J. B. Bossuet, "Preface," No. V, *Histoire des variations des Eglises protestantes,* in *Oeuvres complètes de Bossuet,* ed. F. Lachat (Paris: Louis Vivès, 1883), 14:3.

into and beyond Newman's Oxford days. The First Vatican Council, for example, denied the possibility of any dogmatic development that would involve a transformation of the conceptual meaning of the revealed truth. In *Dei Filius* and in a number of subsequent pronouncements from the magisterium, this argument was explicitly based on a strict reading of chapter 23 of the *Commonitorium*.[28] One could infer, of course, that this teaching implicitly permitted a homogeneous understanding of development that would not involve transformation of the meaning of revelation, and some later neo-scholastics such as Francisco Marín-Sola saw it that way. But Avery Dulles has noted the profoundly conservative intention of this council with regard to the issue of doctrinal development, a position based on a view of revealed truth as a *depositum*, immutable both conceptually and propositionally.[29]

The effects of this conservative interpretation of the Vincentian Canon in the latter part of the nineteenth century were still felt in the major theological debates of the twentieth century. Jesuit Henri Bouillard, for example, maintained that a distinction had to be made between the judgment of faith knowledge, which affirmed an immutable revealed truth, and the ideas or concepts used to repre-

---

[28] *Dei Filius*, chapter 4, in *Decrees of the Ecumenical Councils*, 820 (DS 3020): "Hence, too, that meaning of sacred dogmas is ever to be maintained which has once been declared by holy mother church, and there must never be any abandonment of this sense under the pretext or in the name of a more profound understanding." This is followed by the quotation from chapter 23 of the *Commonitorium* (see *PL* 5:668). On this same point, see *Dei Filius*, canon 4, in *Decrees of the Ecumenical Councils*, 823 (DS 3043): "If anyone says that it is possible that at some time, given the advancement of knowledge, a sense may be assigned to the dogmas propounded by the church which is different from that which the church has understood and understands—*anathema sit.*" See also *Ineffabilis Deus* (1854) (DS 2802), which declares that the church has been given custody of the deposit of faith, and nothing in this deposit is to be changed, either by diminution or addition.

[29] See Dulles, *Survival of Dogma*, 94–95. But Guarino observes: "By citing Vincent's second rule, Vatican I officially admits that dogmatic progress occurs, even though it demands that this progress be homogeneous and genetic, i.e., there must be a fundamental continuity of meaning with what has previously been defined." "Vincent of Lerins and the Hermeneutical Question," 509.

sent such a judgment. These ideas or concepts were subject to the conditions of specific times and were therefore subject to change. Bouillard was challenged by the Dominican followers of M.-J. Garrigou-Lagrange, notably by M. Labourdette, who argued that the concepts used to represent the judgments of faith were as valid as the judgments themselves. This position allowed for virtually no movement in the conceptualization of faith. In contrast, Bouillard's view implied an approach to development that insisted on and began with the immutable revealed truth affirmed in the judgments of faith and then moved toward ever greater conceptual elaboration, conceptual development, and finally, possible change in actual doctrinal language. The Dominican approach, on the other hand, strove toward a delimitation, explication, and refinement of the concepts in which the revealed truth had always been contained and always would be contained.[30]

The most ambitious of the Dominican projects, one that tried to steer a middle course between the Jesuit and Dominican positions, was Francisco Marín-Sola's treatise on the evolution of dogma.[31] Marín-Sola was aware of the significance of Newman's contribution to the discussion and tried to come to terms with it within a scholastic framework. He argued that conceptual development renders explicit what the terminology of logic calls virtual-implicit truths. The only real growth logically allowed would be an internal or intellectual growth in the knowledge of the content of faith, a growth in wisdom and understanding of what had always been taught, everywhere, with the universal consent of the church's bishops and theologians. Such a conceptual development could not readily be translated into the actual practice of faith, or involve change in the

[30] See T. M. Schoof, *A Survey of Catholic Theology: 1800–1970*, trans. N. D. Smith (Paramus, N.J.: Paulist Newman, 1970), 206–7.

[31] Francisco Marín-Sola, *La Evolución homogénea del dogma católico*, 3d ed. (Madrid: Biblioteca de Autores Cristianos, 1952). Marín-Sola explains his title: "To the title of *The Homogeneous Evolution of Dogma* we could have added the subtitle *The Homogeneity of All Catholic Doctrine* in order to indicate that our objective is twofold: First to demonstrate with respect to dogma, properly and strictly speaking, the possibility of true evolution, although always homogeneous evolution; second, to make clear that this evolution is inclusive of all the degrees of Catholic doctrine" (135) (my translation).

outward traditions of church teaching and practice. What Vincent had called *profectus religionis* would become a function of the "mind" of the church. Dogmatic teachings not sharing the frame of mind and conceptual assumptions of earlier formulations would be excluded from authentic *profectus religionis* and were, properly speaking, heresies. Certain logical inferences from established formulations could theoretically be allowed only as long as they did not result in a departure from the interpretations, if not most of the very terminology, of old. Still, some room was left open here for dogmatic development.

Church pronouncements on this issue prior to the Second Vatican Council seemed to come down on the side of the more conservative Dominican approach. In *Humani generis* (1950) Pope Pius XII held that the language of the dogmatic teaching of the church can be perfected and polished (*perfici et perpoliri posse*) by more current philosophical phraseology, but that the ancient concepts of revealed truth must remain unchanged, lest the preservation of dogmatic truth be left to the mercy of philosophical faddism or relativism.[32] These conservative approaches firmly set the limits of the Catholic discussion of dogma and dogmatic change up to the eve of the Second Vatican Council. The truth of revelation was considered to be conceptual in nature and to be given as a *depositum* to the mind of the church. Dogmatic change could not imply substantial change in the conceptual content of faith.[33] The principle of immutability weighed against the acceptability of any theory of dogmatic change that would move beyond a deeper knowledge of the revealed truth contained within the mind of faith. Corresponding

[32] Pope Pius XII, *Humani generis* (DS 3883): "To be sure, all are agreed that the terms representing certain ideas, however much they may have been used in the schools, and even in the authoritative teaching of the Church, are nevertheless susceptible of further perfecting and polishing (*perfici et perpoliri posse*); it is notorious that the Church has not always been consistent in the use of the same identical phrases." English translation from Karl Rahner, ed., *The Teaching of the Catholic Church*, trans. Geoffrey Stevens (Staten Island, N.Y.: Alba House, 1967), 47.

[33] This does not mean that the church failed to recognize the possibility of a virtual and implicit conceptual *development* of the one and same truth which would thereby result in a history of dogma. See Pope Pius XII, *Sempiternus Rex* (1951) (DS 3905), which traces the conceptual development of the church's teaching on Christ from Ephesus to Chalcedon.

verbal change would result only from a logical explication which did not contravene the principle of immutability. The issue of dogmatic change became a problem for the mind of faith because revealed truth and its dogmatic expression were approached as conceptual matter. Only methods appropriate to the composition and analysis of intellectual data, abstracted from historical contingencies, could be admitted into the treatment of dogma. The church's varied experiences of faith and pluralism in the ways that faith is confessed in specific historical contexts remained extraneous to the discussion as long as dogma was approached as conceptual and propositional matter alone and approached within the limits of scholastic theology.

The Second Vatican Council implicitly acknowledged the limitations of this strict reading of the Vincentian Canon by declining to quote the Canon in Article 8 of *Dei Verbum* (*Dogmatic Constitution on Divine Revelation*). Some council participants were concerned that a progressive notion of tradition, in which the church is ever moving toward the fullness of the truth, risked subjecting the revealed truth itself to change. They therefore argued for an inclusion of the Vincentian Canon, which they were interpreting in a restrictive manner. Their request was declined. Joseph Ratzinger, later to become Prefect of the Congregation for the Doctrine of the Faith, explains that one reason was "the dubious light in which this Church writer is now seen by historical research." He elaborates:

> The rejection of the suggestion to include again Vincent de Lérin's well-known text, more or less canonized by two councils is again a step beyond Trent and Vatican I, a productive revision of their texts. . . . It is not that Vatican II is taking back what was intended in those quotations: the rejection of a modernistic evolutionism, an affirmation of the definitive character of the revelation of Christ and the apostolic tradition, to which the Church has nothing to add, but which is its yardstick, but it has another conception of the nature of historical identity and continuity. Vincent of Lérin's static *semper* no longer seems the right way of expressing this problem.[34]

---

[34] Joseph Ratzinger, *Commentary on the Documents of Vatican II*, vol. 3, ed. Herbert Vorgrimler (New York: Herder & Herder, 1969). In light of this judgment made at the Second Vatican Council, it was therefore somewhat noteworthy to see Vincent invoked as recently as October 18, 1995 in the "Responsum ad dubium" to *Ordinatio sacerdotalis* promulgated by the Con-

Indeed, the dynamic pluralism of the confession of faith within specific historical contexts poses a challenge to a strict reading of the Vincentian Canon. It is just such a problem that Newman faced a century earlier in his own situation—how best to read Vincent in order to understand dogma as a source of ecclesial unity.

Newman's Shift to Vincent's "Second Rule"

While Newman tried to remain steadfastly loyal to the Anglican path, several factors gradually turned him to Rome, including his almost reluctant admission that in the Church of Rome an authentic growth in holiness was in fact to be found.[35] But two major factors were to make the shift complete: his realization that the *Via Media* could not be sustained, and the aftermath of his famous "Tract 90."

Newman defended the *Via Media* in several popular pamphlets, or "Tracts." But in 1839 his confidence was shaken by an article written by Nicholas Wiseman, entitled "Anglican Claim to Apostolical Succession," in which Wiseman questioned the authenticity

---

gregation for the Doctrine of the Faith. The Responsum holds that the teaching of *Ordinatio sacerdotalis* "requires definitive assent, since, founded on the written Word of God, and from the beginning constantly preserved and applied in the Tradition of the Church, it has been set forth infallibly by the ordinary and universal Magisterium." The portions emphasized conform to the traditional restrictive reading of Vincent's position. If there be any doubt of the influence of the Vincentian Canon on this teaching, it should be removed by the following sentence, which holds that the Roman Pontiff "has handed on this same teaching by a formal declaration, explicitly stating what is to be held always, everywhere, and by all, as belonging to the deposit of faith." See *Origins* 25 (November 30, 1995): 403.

[35] Newman, *Apologia pro vita sua*, 262. Newman quotes one of his own letters published "on occasion of *Tract 90*: "'The age is moving,' I said, 'towards something; and most unhappily the one religious communion among us, which has of late years been practically in possession of this something, is the Church of Rome. She alone, amid all the errors and evils of her practical system, has given free scope to the feelings of awe, mystery, tenderness, reverence, devotedness, and other feelings which may be especially called Catholic.'"

of the Anglican episcopal succession.[36] While Newman countered Wiseman with an article of his own, Wiseman's appeal to Augustine's Catholic dictum (*securus judicat orbis terrarum*) as a means of determining the authenticity of church doctrine rendered starkly obvious the isolation of the *Via Media* from the life of the church universal. The *Via Media* was tied to the church universal only by tenuous historical arguments, not by virtue of the actual judgment of the whole church, and surely not by any authoritative teaching. If the beliefs of the *Via Media* church seemed to resemble those of the heretical moderate monophysites of the fifth century, Newman argued, then it would appear either that Anglicans too were heretics, or that the Council of Chalcedon was in fact not authoritative.[37] Newman was on the horns of a dilemma.

In that same year, Newman's own analysis of the Council of Chalcedon led him to question the apostolic authenticity of the *Via Media*. Ultimately, Newman felt forced to abandon the Vincentian Canon, which had been so "congenial, or . . . native to the Anglican mind," as the definitive test for authentic teaching and practice. While the Vincentian Canon "takes up a middle position, neither discarding the Fathers nor acknowledging the Pope," problems arose in applying it to particular cases:

> The rule is more serviceable in determining what is not, than what is Christianity! It is irresistible against Protestantism, and in one sense indeed it is irresistible against Rome also, but in the same sense it is irresistible against England. It strikes at Rome through England . . . : if it be narrowed for the purpose of disproving the catholicity of the Creed of Pope Pius, it becomes also an objection to the Athanasian: and if it be relaxed to admit the doctrines retained by the English Church, it no longer excludes certain doctrines of Rome which that Church denies.[38]

In other words, the Canon could cut either way, and the *quod semper,*

[36] Ibid., 218–19.

[37] Ibid., 217.

[38] Newman, *Essay*, 11. See Owen Chadwick, *From Bossuet to Newman: The Idea of Doctrinal Development* (Cambridge: University Press, 1957), 121: "Between the authority of the Church and agnosticism he could see no standing ground; and for him the authority of the Church was null apart from that authority of antiquity which the Vincentian Canon had so laconically summarized."

quod ubique, quod ab omnibus was therefore useless for purposes of settling Newman's dilemma.

But this still left Vincent's second rule, the one that offered an organic metaphor for development. This Newman would keep in mind in the events that followed. For Newman's precarious Anglican balance was upset with the publication of "Tract 90" in February 1841, in which he scrutinized the Thirty-Nine Articles of the Anglican Church, which had been drawn up as a kind of theological compromise under Elizabeth I. Newman wanted to show that the Articles were not Protestant in implication, but that they reflected the pre-Tridentine sense of the church, and to answer the claim that "there are in the Articles propositions or terms inconsistent with the Catholic faith." For "it is a *duty* which we owe both to the Catholic Church and to our own, to take our reformed confessions in the most Catholic sense they will admit. . . . The Protestant Confession was drawn up with the purpose of including Catholics; and Catholics now will not be excluded."[39] Why did Newman take this position? As Wilfrid Ward correctly observed, "Newman had gone to history. He had realised that the Articles were a compromise, and that their framers had hoped to get the Catholic party to subscribe to them in spite of their Protestant rhetoric."[40] The ensuing uproar, during which "Tract 90" was condemned by the Anglican bishops, shattered Newman, who had only intended to produce an irenical treatise designed to counter arguments in favor of switching over to Rome; he had hardly intended to argue for the plausibility of giving up the Church of England in favor of Rome.

With the rejection of his reading of the Thirty-Nine Articles, Newman felt he had no choice but to retreat, and on February 2, 1843, the Feast of the Purification, he preached his famous sermon entitled "The Theory of Developments in Religious Doctrine," also known as the Fifteenth Oxford University Sermon.[41] On September 18, 1843, he resigned his Anglican ministry and moved from Oxford to nearby Littlemore. At Littlemore, he focused on whether

[39] Newman, "Tract 90: Remarks on Certain Passages in the Thirty-Nine Articles," in *Tracts for the Times* (Oxford: J. Vincent, 1842), vol. 6, 80–82.

[40] Wilfrid Ward, *The Life of John Henry Cardinal Newman*, 2 vols. (New York: Longmans, 1912), vol. 1, 72.

[41] Newman, "Sermon XV: The Theory of Developments in Religious Doctrine," in *Newman's University Sermons*, 312–51.

there is "a possible reconciliation between the claims of the Catholic Church and the autonomy of historical science."[42] That is, could dogmatic change be squared with an unchanging content of faith? He proceeded to work out his theory of dogmatic development which we now know as the *Essay*.

Newman's mind and heart had turned to Rome. What he saw there was a church whose image more closely resembled the image of the apostolic church than did any post-Reformation church, including the Church of England or the *Via Media*.

> On the whole, all parties will agree that, of all existing systems, the present communion of Rome is the nearest approximation in fact to the Church of the Fathers possible though some may think it to be nearer still to that Church on paper. Did St. Athanasius or St. Ambrose come suddenly to life, it cannot be doubted what communion he would (we will say) mistake for his own.[43]

Not only does the historical evidence bear this out; more importantly, it is only reasonable to assume this to be the case.

> Till positive reasons grounded on facts are adduced to the contrary, the most natural hypothesis . . . is to consider that the society of Christians, which the Apostles left on earth, were of that religion to which the Apostles had converted them. . . . It is not a violent assumption, then, but rather mere abstinence from the wanton admission of a principle which would necessarily lead to the most vexatious and preposterous scepticism, to take it for granted, before proof to the contrary, that the Christianity of the second, fourth, seventh, twelfth, sixteenth, and intermediate centuries is in its substance the very religion which Christ and His Apostles taught in the first.[44]

It remained only to demonstrate the plausibility of this "abstinence" from skepticism.

But this would not be easy. The Roman Church of the nineteenth century was the obvious result of a long process of changes; it held doctrines and engaged in practices which the apostolic church did not obviously share. So Newman was faced with a difficulty: He

---

[42] Gustave Weigel, "Foreword" to Newman, *An Essay on the Development of Christian Doctrine,* 1878 rev. ed., 9.

[43] Newman, *Essay*, 90.

[44] Ibid., 5.

firmly believed that the Church of Rome did embody the authentic apostolic faith and that there was ample evidence in favor of that conviction. But he could not deny that significant changes had taken place between the first centuries of the church and the nineteenth century, changes weighty enough to cast doubts on the apostolic authenticity of the Roman Church. The solution: "an hypothesis [of development] to account for a difficulty."[45] For if, following a strict reading of Vincent, no development in teaching and practice were to be granted even to the church which embodied the authentic apostolic faith, then no modern church at all could validly claim apostolic authenticity. But such a conclusion would be unacceptable, for there was ample evidence that authentic apostolic faith was thriving in the Roman Church. A key theological motivation for Newman's work on development, at least in the *Essay*, was the theoretical justification of this assumption. Newman could thereby render plausible the notion that obvious divergences from the teaching and practices of the primitive church that are found in the Roman Church do not constitute a perversion of the authentic apostolic faith, but rather are signs of organic growth of a universal faith.[46]

To Newman's mind, there was no compelling theological or historical reason to reject the hypothesis of growth or development in the teaching and practice of the church. Such a hypothesis would not imply the mutability of revealed truth but, following Vincent's second rule, would in fact assume the constant and unchanging identity of revealed truth; only the "idea" in which it is held by the church would develop. And a glance at the historical data points to the fact that dogmatic development has occurred; it is a fact of life. Even the church most faithful to the apostolic faith could be expected to bear the marks of some dogmatic development. But the development of dogmatic propositions to be found in this church would not constitute a radical rupture with apostolic teaching and practice. Its dogmatic development would not compromise the identity of the one revealed truth as it was understood by the apostolic church in teaching and practice.[47] In all of this Newman was

[45] Ibid., 28.

[46] Nicholas Lash, *Change in Focus: A Study of Doctrinal Change and Continuity* (London: Sheed & Ward, 1973), 115.

[47] See Chadwick, *From Bossuet to Newman*, 144: "The argument is not

arguing a position much in the spirit of interpreting the Vincentian Canon in light of Vincent's second rule.[48] Some kind of organic development of the faith tradition had taken place, not only in the teaching of faith but in its confession as well. This insight would lead to an elaboration of the notion of dogma itself in relation to something more fundamental, the "idea" of Christianity.

NEWMAN'S "IDEA" AND ITS DEVELOPMENT

Newman's famous work on dogma is called an essay on the development of *doctrine*.[49] The use of this term should not suggest that Newman was concerned only with the development of dogmatic statements, even though he was a strong proponent of the need for an infallible developing authority and of the indispensable role played by what he called "the dogmatic principle" in the church, whereby the church maintains "consistency and thoroughness in its teaching."[50] But doctrine includes more than authoritative teaching; it includes the entire spectrum of church practice, from the teaching function of the episcopacy to the pious veneration of the saints. Newman's field of data excluded in principle no aspect of the life of faith, doctrinal (belief and teaching) or confessional (the practices of faith in worship and deed). Newman's broad use of "doctrine" was consonant with the broader ancient sense of dogma described earlier in this book. It included, but was not exhausted by, authoritatively taught dogmatic statements.

'History shows that change has occurred: therefore we must adopt mutability instead of immutability as a general principle'. The argument is 'The less mutability has occurred the truer is the modern church, but since history shows that *some* mutability has occurred, even in the least mutable of churches, we need a theory.'"

[48] See especially Newman's citation of Vincent's "law of the body" (*Essay*, 159) as an illustration of the first note of authentic development, "preservation of type." See also Guarino, "Vincent of Lerins and the Hermeneutical Question," 496.

[49] According to Newman, dogmas are "supernatural truths irrevocably committed to human language, imperfect because it is human, but definitive and necessary because given from above." *Essay*, 303.

[50] Ibid., 329.

Doctrine expresses the "idea of Christianity," which lives in the mind of the church. Changes in doctrine are changes in the representation of the idea, which itself organically unfolds and exfoliates as the church lives and changes within history. The idea of Christianity was originally formed when the church received revelation within particular historical circumstances. Revelation is analogous to a sensory impression, and like the object of sensory experience, is communicated by God as an objective but supernatural datum to the church as subject.[51] Christianity came into the world not as an institution but as a result of a *sacred* impression which, when received, became known as a sacred idea.[52] While a distinction can therefore be made between revelation and the reception of it, a unity exists between the revelation which impressed itself on the mind of the church and the idea of it held by the minds of the faithful. The sacred content of the idea, the "truth" of revelation, is inseparable from the idea itself. Revelation lives on, and is continually communicated, in and through the "idea" of Christianity. Lash explains:

> For Newman, a "real idea" is not sharply differentiated, ontologically, from the "object" which it "represents": it is that object, as perceived, apprehended, grasped, in the life and thought of a society. . . . The unity of the "idea," as of the "object," is taken for granted.[53]

The idea takes on a life of its own within the mind of faith, "which proceeds to investigate it, and to draw it forth in successive and distinct sentences."[54] This mind of the church, a union of minds, hearts, and lives, materializes within and is defined by the living history of faith in the church. The "idea" is the grace-given content of the sacred impression made upon this mind of the church, a content that can become explicit knowledge and which can develop. The dogmatic proposition "expressive of the judgments which the mind forms, or the impressions which it receives, of Revealed Truth," is but one result of the development of the idea of Christianity within the mind of the church.[55]

[51] Newman, "Sermon XV," 320.
[52] Newman, *Essay*, 71.
[53] Lash, *Change in Focus*, 91. See also Newman, *Essay*, 76.
[54] Newman, "Sermon XV," 320.
[55] Ibid.

Authentic dogmatic development, as opposed to a deviation from the original idea, is the unfolding of the idea of Christianity into its many aspects, which are then regrouped into new ideas. The mind of the church is not abstracted from history. It is a historical mind, molded and infused by historical factors such as culture, language, and human events. The idea lives in the mind of the church, not as suprahistorical truth but as historically conditioned truth. The idea itself develops as the life of faith develops in history; but like the child who grows into an adult in Vincent's analogy, the ontological identity of this truth persists unimpaired through all stages of historical development. The idea of Christianity therefore develops organically within the mind of the church because it is part of the content of that mind which itself grows, expands, and changes throughout the course of the historical life of the church.[56] And the idea of Christianity develops in a variety of ways, all of which can result in new doctrine. These include political and historical developments, where the role of abstract reason can be very small.[57] What these types of development have in common is not the function of abstract reason but the basic principles or elements of Christian faith (e.g., the Incarnation of God in Jesus Christ) from which these developments emerge.

Aim and Method of Newman's Essay

Since the aim of the *Essay* derives from the problem of conflict between historical testimony and faith claims, historical evidences play a major role in the *Essay*'s method. The aim of the *Essay* is to be distinguished from that of the earlier Fifteenth Oxford University Sermon. The aim of "Sermon XV" was, in Newman's words, "to investigate the connection between Faith and Dogmatic Confession

---

[56] This interpretation of Newman runs counter to that of J.-H. Walgrave, who claims that development in Newman is a characteristic of abstract knowledge, and that Newman's "idea" parallels Aquinas's *verbum mentis*. The similarities are superficial. Walgrave's reading is based on the premise that the *Essay* is a search for the right means of arguing for development according to the principles of consciousness, and then testing these means from the standpoint of reason. See Walgrave, *Newman: Le développement du dogme* (Tournai: Casterman, 1956), 106 n. 8, and 33–34.

[57] Newman, *Essay*, 38–50.

... and to show the office of the Reason in reference to it."[58] In this sermon Newman explains that the development of faith from the reception of revelation to the articulation of it in creed and dogma is like the move of the mind from implicit to explicit forms of reasoning. This sermon actually extends to the framework of dogmatic development a problem for faith which he had addressed three years earlier in the Thirteenth Oxford University Sermon, "Implicit and Explicit Reason." In this sermon, he declared:

> Nothing would be more theoretical and unreal than to suppose that true Faith cannot exist except when molded upon a Creed, and based upon Evidence; yet nothing would indicate a more shallow philosophy than to say that it ought carefully to be disjoined from dogmatic and argumentative statements. To assert the latter is to discard the science of theology from the service of Religion; to assert the former, is to maintain that every child, every peasant, must be a theologian. . . . And I will add that, if there is a question, the intrusion of which may be excused in the present age, and to which the mind is naturally led . . . it is the relation of Faith to Reason under the Gospel.[59]

The aim of "Sermon XV" is therefore to put forth more than a hypothesis to account for a difficulty; it is to put forth a theoretical explanation of the relationship between states of faith consciousness and the rational articulation of these states. Yet even "Sermon XV," with its focus on reason and an aim narrower than that of the *Essay*, tells us that the "secondary and intelligible means by which we receive the Divine Verities" include scriptural meditation, study, prayer, and significantly, personal exposure to people "themselves in possession of the sacred ideas."[60] Development of the idea of Christianity may occur with the assistance of reason, but ultimately it is an event of a living faith "which extends into mystery." The *Essay*, as we have seen, is motivated in part by the fact that the claims of faith and the testimony of history do not always or obviously support each other. Thus, the *Essay* is aimed "towards a solution of the difficulty which has been stated,—the difficulty, as far as it exists, which lies in the way of our using in controversy the testimony of

[58] Newman, "Sermon XV," 319.
[59] John Henry Newman, "Sermon XIII: Implicit and Explicit Reason," in *Newman's University Sermons,* 253–55.
[60] Newman, "Sermon XV," 333.

our most natural informant concerning the doctrine and worship of Christianity, viz., the history of eighteen hundred years."[61]

But the evidences of this history do not stand as brute facts in opposition to faith. They take on a coherent meaning only within the framework of the "antecedent probability" that they will help to accomplish what the *Essay* aims to accomplish. The term "antecedent probability" is unique to Newman's lexicon. The word "probability" refers to the convergence of the mind toward a judgment reached through a process of induction. In David Hume, such induction is limited to the field of sensory experience and our memory or ideas of it. We can be apodictically certain only of that which comes through sensory impressions. Belief is "a lively idea related to or associated with a present impression," which requires a predisposition toward the evidence such that it becomes the basis of lively ideational content.[62] Newman was confident that the evidence of history would, when submitted to the inductive methods of historical inquiry, yield judgments as certain as those also reached in the physical sciences through inductive methods. "And thus a converging evidence in favour of certain doctrines, may, under circumstances, be as clear a proof of their Apostolical origin as can be reached practically from the *Quod semper, quod ubique, quod ab omnibus.*"[63]

Thus, in the *Essay* Newman adopted the inductive method ("first, an imperfect, secondly, a growing evidence, thirdly, in consequence a delayed inference and judgment, fourthly, reasons producible to account for the delay"). But he added a crucial dimension: the predisposition to believe. Just as in matters of faith we bring a predisposition to believe to the "evidence" of revelation (for example, to scripture) so that we can make certain judgments about the content of revelation, so too in understanding how the idea of this revelation develops, we bring antecedent judgments to bear on the evidences such that the probabilities otherwise reached by induction

[61] Newman, *Essay*, 28. See also Nicholas Lash, "The Notions of 'Implicit' and 'Explicit' Reason in Newman's University Sermons: A Difficulty," *Heythrop Journal* 11 (1970): 51–52.

[62] See David Hume, *Treatise of Human Nature*, ed. Ernest C. Mossner (Baltimore: Pelican, 1969), I.iii.7, p. 144.

[63] Newman, *Essay*, 114.

square with the predisposition of the mind of faith. For example, Newman argued in chapter 2 of the *Essay* that given the plausibility of development as an explanation for change in Christian doctrine, and given the fact that ideas develop, then an antecedent presumption may be made that Christian doctrine develops and that an inductive approach to the evidence will support this. The antecedent probability of development takes into account both an inductive approach to the evidence and the predisposition of faith that such development is a matter of providence and is within the intention of the mind of God. Both of these lines converge in the firm conviction that dogmatic development is a feature of the history of Christianity.

The Meanings of "Development"

Newman was explicit about his use of the word "development" in the *Essay*. First he noted three fundamental and legitimate meanings of the word: the process of development, the result of the process, and either authentic (true) or inauthentic (false) results.[64] But Newman also explicitly excluded certain senses of the word as inappropriate to the discussion of dogmatic development. For example, mathematical developments are not properly analogous to dogmatic developments because mathematical developments "are conducted on strict demonstration; and the conclusions in which they terminate, being necessary, cannot be declensions from the original idea."[65] Mathematical developments are properly analytic rather than synthetic. But developments in the Christian creed and ritual are subject to the influence of concrete historical factors, and the outcome of such a process of development is by no means predictable, necessary, or contained in the point of departure: it is subject both to the caprices of human history and to the divine intention.

Several types of development are germane to the discussion of the development of dogma. Newman distinguished five different types of development through which development of the idea of Christianity has occurred: political, logical, historical, ethical, and

[64] Ibid., 38.
[65] Ibid., 38–39.

metaphysical.[66] Political developments have resulted in ecclesial social structures such as the episcopate. Logical developments, which involve the use of reason but not necessarily formal logical deduction, have resulted in theological conclusions, some of which have later been authoritatively taught, as, for example, the *Theotokos* doctrine of the Council of Ephesus (431). Historical developments, where judgments once confined to a few people are spread by way of historical events to a larger community, have resulted in such catholic additions to tradition as the canonical status of formerly provincial New Testament books and the canonization by the universal church of local saints. Ethical developments are the result of the transition from doctrine into worship, as in the transition from the teachings of the Gospels and of Paul on the eucharist into the liturgy and theology of the mass. By metaphysical development Newman referred specifically to the process of analyzing ideas and organizing the results of this analysis into a body of dogmatic statements. Such dogmas would include original sin, the real presence of Christ in the eucharist, and justification, each of which "is but the expression of the inward belief of Catholics on these several points, formed upon an analysis of that belief."[67]

Newman's belief that dogmatic development is in part the process and result of the metaphysical development of the idea of Christianity does not mean that development is abstracted from the life of faith as it is realized in history. The development of "creed" and "ritual" and of dogmatic statements themselves issues from the historical life of the idea in the mind of the church, from the confession of faith that occurs through concrete events, linguistic factors, and cultural influences. This entanglement in history is even more evident in the types of development which Newman specified in addition to metaphysical developments. He devoted much of his discussion in the *Essay* to the political development of the idea of Christianity, a type of development subject to the most finite and material of historical factors, resulting in the changing forms of the episcopacy and its exercise in the history of the church. On the basis of his discussion of the political development of Christianity one can understand the influence of historical factors on the other types of development, including metaphysical development:

[66] Ibid., 39–50.
[67] Newman, "Sermon XV," 320.

The above sketch . . . is only part of what might be set down in evidence of the wonderful identity of type which characterizes the Catholic Church from the first to last. I have confined myself for the most part to the political aspect; but a parallel illustration might be drawn simply from her doctrinal, or from her devotional.[68]

Metaphysical development, which results in dogmatic propositions and even in defined truths of faith, is but one aspect of the historical life of the idea of Christianity. "One aspect of Revelation must not be allowed to exclude or to obscure another; and Christianity is dogmatical, devotional, practical all at once."[69]

The Immutability of Revealed Truth

Although the idea of Christianity develops as an object of knowledge in organic connection with the historical life of the church, the truth of revelation itself, the content of the idea, does not itself change.[70] Newman safeguarded the immutability of revealed truth while arguing for a real change or development in the idea to which that truth is by nature bound. This was not an argument for mere verbal change in doctrinal formulae, but for the quasi-organic unfolding of the idea itself. It is as if the idea were a seed which carried the immutable genetic message that directed its growth into a tree: a real unfolding occurs, but the "truth" of the idea remains self-identical through all stages of the unfolding, just as the genetic code is passed on intact to the tree and its progeny.

But the organic metaphor, like any good metaphor, both functions and falters, for the idea of Christianity has no "genetic" code. Its unfolding is not simply organic; in fact it occurs through both the continuities and the discontinuities of the historical life of the church. The basis for an identity-through-change is found in the several principles of faith that are given with revelation, not least among them the Incarnation.[71] These principles "are assumptions

---

[68] Newman, *Essay*, 300.
[69] Ibid., 34.
[70] Ibid., 51.
[71] Ibid., 165ff., 301ff.

rather than objective professions" and stand as the permanent basis for the development of the idea of Christianity.[72] Examples of such principles include sacramentality, the efficacy of grace, the malignancy of sin, and the very necessity of verbal dogma. Development itself is a principle of Christian faith.[73] These principles not only provide continuity between the doctrines of one age of faith and another, but guarantee that the truth of revelation remains changeless despite development of the idea of Christianity. Newman could therefore say with meaning and conviction that the idea "changes in order to remain the same."[74]

Newman's emphasis on the immutability of these principles of faith enabled him to argue for the development of new dogmatic forms, not merely reformulation or even new understanding of the old. There is a real development in the revealed idea of Christianity. In "Sermon XV" this development is explained by the fact that the church has at times been unaware of some aspects of the idea of Christianity and has only later defined them. What was once held implicitly by the church was later made explicit. The development of aspects of the idea of Christianity from implicit to explicit stages has even resulted in the genesis of new ideas that were ultimately derived from the original one. For example, Newman maintained that as a result of the Apollinarian and Monophysite controversies, "texts descriptive of created mediation ceased to belong to our Lord, so was room opened for created mediators." The development of the doctrine of the church concerning the human and divine natures of Christ thus "became the natural introduction to the *cultus Sanctorum*."[75] This "birth of an idea, the development, in explicit form, of what was already latent within it," occurs against the backdrop of the sacred "impression" which is not only the "content" of the original idea but the source of the changeless principles of faith.[76]

[72] Ibid., 167.
[73] Ibid., 303–4.
[74] Ibid., 38.
[75] Ibid., 128.
[76] Newman, "Sermon XV," 321.

CONSENSUS FIDELIUM

Newman's developmental approach to dogma provides a solution to the problem Vincent's Canon posed to generations of theologians: how to account for the change that was so obvious in dogma without compromising the immutability of the revealed truth. But this solution was tied to an equally strong interest on Newman's part in understanding dogma as a function of the life of the church as a whole. Dogma functions as an instrument of unity, the expression of a consensus of faith. But Newman was very careful in his elaboration of this idea.

Although the idea of Christianity is a historical truth, Newman found the notion of the organic development of an idea in the mind of the church to be the most fitting analogy for the development of the faith tradition. The idea of Christianity lives not only as an object impressed upon the mind, but as the expanding content of the mind that has appropriated it. It has both objective and subjective status: objective in the sense that the idea remains itself despite development; subjective in that it is "the subject-matter of exercises of the reason" in the minds of Christians. Our question here is how the idea maintains both objective and subjective status in the mind of the church.

The Idea in the Mind of the Church

In many parts of the *Essay* Newman drew a parallel between the mind of an individual and that of wider society.[77] One can learn from these references that a single idea lives in or takes possession of many minds, but that this single idea is viewed differently by each person in whom it lives.

> The idea which represents an object or supposed object is commensurate with the sum total of its possible aspects, however they may vary in the separate consciousness of individuals; and in proportion to the variety of aspects under which it represents itself to various minds is its force and depth, and the argument for its reality.[78]

[77] Newman, *Essay*, sections 2.1.1–2; 5.4.1; 5.5.2; and 9.0.1.
[78] Ibid., 32. See also *Essay*, 68: "Development is not an effect of wishing

How do we move from this notion, of an idea living in "the separate consciousness of individuals," to the notion that it lives in the mind of a society or in the mind of the church? Newman did not offer a theory so much as a description of the way an idea lives simultaneously in many minds, ultimately in the mind of a society. The idea achieves its maturity when it becomes the "common property" of many minds.

> The multitude of opinions formed concerning it . . . will be collected, compared, sorted, sifted, selected, rejected, gradually attached to it, separated from it, in the minds of individuals and of the community. It will, in proportion to its native vigour and subtlety, introduce itself into the framework and details of social life, changing public opinion, and strengthening or undermining the foundations of established order.[79]

Even in its subjective state of possession by many minds, the idea retains what both Lash and Walgrave have called a quasi-Platonic status.[80] The nature of the idea itself, with its "native vigour and subtlety" insinuating itself into many minds and ultimately into "social life," is the basis for the transposition in Newman's argument from the mind of the individual to the mind of the church.

> Thus in time it will . . . after all be little more than the proper representative of one idea, being in substance what that idea meant from the first, its complete image as seen in a combination of diversified aspects, with the suggestions and corrections of many minds, the illustration of many experiences.[81]

But this description of the life of an idea raises another question. It is one thing to say that the idea that motivates Christian faith realizes itself socially; it is another to say that this social realization takes

---

and resolving, or of forced enthusiasm, or of any mechanism of reasoning, or of any mere subtlety of intellect; but comes of its own innate power of expansion within the mind in its season, though with the use of reflection and argument and original thought, more or less as it may happen, with a dependence on the ethical growth of the mind itself, and with a reflex influence upon it."

[79] Ibid., 35.

[80] Lash, *Newman on Development*, 51; see also Walgrave, *Newman: Le développement du dogme*, 171ff.

[81] Newman, *Essay*, 35.

place within the mind of the church.[82] How do we determine what this mind of the church is?

Conspiratio Pastorum et Fidelium

Newman and others in the nineteenth century often used "consciousness" (i.e., mind or self-awareness) to speak of the *sensus fidei Ecclesiae.* "Tradition would be the consciousness of the Church, and that according to two aspects, subjective and objective, corresponding to act or faculty, and to content."[83] The basis for arguing from the mind of the individual to the mind of the church is not the objectivity of the "idea" but the nature of the church itself. Faith lives in and is transmitted through the *sensus fidei* that is shared by all the faithful who constitute the church. In order to determine the mind of the church, we need first to determine how the individual person shares in this *sensus fidei Ecclesiae.* Apart from the obvious theological basis for such a sharing found in baptism and the practice of faith, the individual Christian participates in a a *conspiratio pastorum et fidelium,* a union of pastors and faithful, teachers and taught. This refers to a delicately balanced relationship between the teaching function of the church and the role of the faithful as a whole in arriving at an explicit knowledge of the content of faith.[84]

In a famous article of July 1859 entitled "On Consulting the Faithful in Matters of Doctrine," Newman explained that the tradition of the apostles has been committed to the entire church as a singular unifying reality [*per modum unius*], but through different means in different times and places: "sometimes by the mouth of the episcopacy, sometimes by the doctors, sometimes by the people, sometimes by liturgies, rites, ceremonies and customs, by events, disputes, movements, and all those other phenomena which

---

[82] Lash, "Notions of 'Implicit' and 'Explicit' Reason," 49: "The ambiguity in the fifteenth sermon . . . concerns the legitimacy of extrapolating the notion of an 'implicit *starting point*' from the descriptive psychology of the individual to a theory of doctrinal development."

[83] Congar, *La Tradition et les traditions*, vol. 2, *Essai théologique*, 85, 293 n. 43 (my translation).

[84] For a further specification of Newman's use of this term, see Congar, *La Tradition et les traditions*, vol. 1, *Essai historique*, 261.

are comprised under the name of history."[85] The channels of tradition are many and diverse. They are not limited to what we now call ordinary teachings, to dogmas (defined or not), nor even to that which could be adequately conceptualized. These are the means by which the idea of Christianity becomes incarnated and develops in the faith of the church. But of equal importance is the way the idea of Christianity is taught and transmitted. "It follows that none of these channels of tradition may be treated with disrespect; granting at the same time fully, that the gift of discerning, discriminating, defining, promulgating, and enforcing any portion of that tradition resides solely in the *Ecclesia docens*."[86]

Reflected in this article are the antecedent probabilities that Newman had specified earlier in the *Essay*: the development of the idea of Christianity and an infallible teaching authority. And while it is possible on the basis of these statements to conclude that the hierarchical magisterium plays an exclusive role in the specification and transmission of the content of faith, Newman situated this role and established the authority of the magisterium itself within the context of the living instinct for faith possessed by all the faithful, not only teaching authorities.[87] The evidence of history bears this out. In his study of history, Newman was troubled that he "could not find certain portions of the defined doctrine of the Church in ecclesiastical writers. . . . Up to the date of the definition of certain articles of doctrine respectively, there was so very deficient evidence from existing documents that Bishops, doctors, theologians held them."[88] In *The Arians of the Fourth Century*, Newman reached the bold conclusion that the faithful, with their "instinct" for faith (the *sensus fidelium*), and not the institution of the magisterium vested in the bishops, had maintained the faith catholic in the aftermath of the Arian controversy:

> The episcopate, whose action was so prompt and concordant at Nicea on the rise of Arianism, did not, as a class or order of men, play a good part in the troubles consequent upon the Council; and

[85] Newman, *On Consulting the Faithful*, 163.

[86] Ibid.

[87] It seems that Walgrave exaggerates the role that the magisterium actually plays in Newman's model. See Walgrave, *Newman: Le développement du dogma*, 180–81.

[88] Newman, *On Consulting the Faithful*, 63–64.

the laity did. The Catholic people, in the length and breadth of Christendom, were the obstinate champions of Catholic truth, and the bishops were not.[89]

Wishing to avoid a simplistic distinction between clerical teachers and nonclerical learners, Newman extended the term "faithful" to the entire church, but still gave great weight to the role of the *ecclesia discens:*

> [I]n speaking of the laity, I speak inclusively of their parish-priests (so to call them), at least in many places; but on the whole, taking a wide view of the history, we are obliged to say that the governing body of the Church came short, and the governed were pre-eminent in faith, zeal, courage, and constancy.[90]

Nevertheless, each part of the church, teaching and learning, has a distinct role to play. The magisterium may have the sole teaching role in the church and it may even be "distinct from, and independent of tradition," but it is "never in fact separated from it." The magisterium, which in the nineteenth century as in our own was claimed as one of the sure notes of catholic unity, is situated here within the living instinct for faith possessed by all the faithful and not apart from it or even formally prior to it. For the living faith tradition is transmitted not merely by the teaching of the magisterium but through the *sensus fidelium Ecclesiae*, which is discovered in the *conspiratio* of both teaching authorities and the body of the faithful. Such a *conspiratio* of teachers and taught led to the declaration of the Immaculate Conception in 1854, where "the Church teaching and the Church taught" joined together in confessing the faith.[91]

The Church Teaching and Learning

The position taken by Newman on consulting the faithful marks a significant advance in his thinking. In an earlier work, *Lectures on the*

[89] Newman, "Appendix," note V, "The Orthodoxy of the Body of the Faithful during the Supremacy of Arianism," in *The Arians of the Fourth Century*, 5th ed. (London: Pickering, 1883), 445. Newman reviews the entire "Appendix" in *On Consulting the Faithful*, 77–101.

[90] Newman, *Arians*, 445.

[91] Newman, *On Consulting the Faithful*, 71.

Prophetical Office (1837), the idea of *conspiratio* had not yet matured. Instead, he distinguished between the prophetic and the episcopal (or apostolic) tradition: the process of development occurred in the prophetic; the result was incorporated into the episcopal.[92] He abandoned this distinction in "Sermon XV," where instead his language shifted to near identification of the mind of the church with "the secret life of millions of faithful souls."[93] In *On Consulting the Faithful*, both process and result of development are rooted in the church's consciousness of faith. Newman considered it important to make his argument as he did in this article, for Ultramontanist (pro-papal) fever was in high pitch in 1859 and threatened to eclipse the legitimate role of the faithful of the local churches in the transmission and articulation of the faith in centers far from Rome. Apart from France, no place reflected the stresses and strains within the church over the exercise of papal authority more than England, and it could be argued that few people suffered through this period more than did Newman and the Oxford converts.[94]

Newman's interest in the *sensus fidelium* and the *conspiratio pastorum et fidelium*, therefore, was not merely an academic exercise. The occasion of this interest, a dispute with Bishop Ullathorne over the

[92] *Lectures on the Prophetical Office of the Church, Viewed Relatively to Romanism and Popular Protestantism* (London: Rivington, 1837). At this early stage, Newman's thinking reflected his respect for the Vincentian Canon: "The highest evidence of Apostolical Tradition is where the testimony is not only everywhere and always, but where it has ever been recognized **as** tradition, and reflected upon and professedly delivered down as saving, by those who hold it" (295). He distinguishes here between the "Episcopal Tradition," which is the authoritative teaching of doctrine, and the "Prophetical Tradition, existing primarily in the bosom of the Church itself. . . . This is obviously of a very different kind from the Episcopal Tradition, yet in its origin it is equally Apostolical . . ." (298–99). Such a distinction allows him more ably to argue for the apostolic nature of the Church of England, which is a principal aim at this stage in his thinking about a *Via Media* between Roman Catholicism and Anglicanism.

[93] Newman, "Sermon XV," 323.

[94] See John Coulson's introduction to *On Consulting the Faithful*, 1–20. For a discussion of Ultramontanism, the subsequent rise of Modernism, and the complex relation of Newman's thought to each, see Marvin R. O'Connell, *Critics on Trial: An Introduc2tion to the Catholic Modernist Crisis* (Washington, D.C.: Catholic University of America, 1994).

proper role of the laity in education, was historically quite specific. But the dispute raised for Newman a deeper theological question about the relationship between the laity and the church, and finally about the nature of the church itself. Later, in the "Newman-Perrone Paper," Newman was to argue that the possession by individuals of revealed truth, called here the "Word of God," could be applied to the church as a whole. The laity as well as the episcopacy witness to their own understanding of the faith tradition and thus contribute to the ongoing transmission of God's Word.[95] The church continues to receive and to know the truth of faith to the degree that the instinct of faith, possessed by all the faithful, assists in faithfully transmitting the faith.[96]

This activity of transmitting the faith is the human foundation of the "mind" of the church. As this mind of the church becomes more explicitly known and universally shared in the *conspiratio pastorum et fidelium,* a basis emerges for authoritative teaching of the truth of faith by the magisterium and for the confession of faith in various forms. In this *conspiratio,* the teachers become learners, and the learners become teachers. The entire church is inspired to transmit the faith as a living tradition, and this tradition includes the developing doctrinal formulations of faith. Thus, the idea of Christianity develops organically in the mind of the church because it develops in the lives of the faithful as they continue to experience it in various places and come to understand it. Dogma captures this idea in history, is subject to appropriation by the faithful as part of the "mind of the church," and through the *conspiratio pastorum et fidelium,* serves as an instrument of unity.

After expanding the notion of dogma, Newman therefore early on laid out two principles for all further discussion of dogma: an understanding of church within which dogma functions as the expression of a unity of consensus, and a model of faith transmission that preserves the truth of revelation even as it transmits it through an array of changing dogmatic expressions. Still, he wrote

[95] Samuel D. Femiano, *Infallibility of the Laity: The Legacy of Newman* (New York, N.Y.: Herder & Herder, 1967), 42–44, 50.

[96] For an earlier discussion of the importance of the *sensus fidelium* in Newman's approach to the unifying function of dogma, see Paul Crowley, "Catholicity, Inculturation and Newman's *Sensus Fidelium,*" *Heythrop Journal* 33 (1992): 161–74.

before the emergence of a truly pluralistic church and the thorny questions raised by the proliferation of local churches in non-European cultures. It would remain for later theologians to lift Newman's accomplishment from its organic developmental framework and place it in the context of philosophical and theological systems reflective of modern pluralism. One of the most important of these attempts was undertaken by Karl Rahner.

CHAPTER 3

Dogma as Symbol of Faith

[W]hat I mean is this: how, within this Church, a binding unity of faith and a new way of functioning [can] be developed by its magisterium on the one hand and on the other a pluralism of theology and interpretations of the one and binding faith. . . .

—Karl Rahner[1]

Newman shared the nineteenth-century stage with another Briton, Charles Darwin, who also composed a theory of organic change. And like Darwin's theory, the general lines of Newman's theory have withstood the tests of time. It has established a mainstream paradigm within which dogma's function and development can be understood and obvious change can be reconciled with the ancient principle of the immutability of revealed truth. But like the notion of selection that drives Darwin's theory, the fundamental organic metaphor in Newman's theory of a continuous development can be critically appraised. "Progress" is by no means accepted today as much as it was in the nineteenth century, as a quasi law of nature. In fact, the twentieth century has seen a general discrediting of the idea of progress as a product of the optimism of the early modern period that is now coming to a close.[2] This

---

[1] Karl Rahner, "Unity of the Church—Unity of Mankind," in *Theological Investigations*, vol. 20, trans. Edward Quinn (New York: Crossroad, 1981), 169.

[2] See, e.g., Stephen Toulmin, *Cosmopolis: The Hidden Agenda of Modernity* (Chicago: University of Chicago Press, 1990); and Louis Dupré, *Passage to*

questioning of progressive development was part of the self-questioning of modernity itself as the world became perceived as a less cohesive place. In the modern period, the sources of cohesion and order and continuity would be sought not so much in overarching organic and developmental structures as in the ontological structures of the human person. This would mark the great turn from the objective laws of nature to the ontological composition of the human subject.

In the early stages of this questioning of the philosophical tenets of pre-modernity Karl Rahner (1904–1984) proposed an approach to dogma that would stand in critical relation to Newman's earlier treatment of dogma. Rahner stood at the crossroads of two major paths of thought: the theological tradition of Thomas Aquinas and the philosophical tradition of phenomenology, particularly the transcendental work of Martin Heidegger, which owed so much to Immanuel Kant's analysis of the transcendental structures of the knowing human subject. In general terms, the transcendental approach attempts to lay out the fundamental metaphysical structures of a human being that enable any human person to come to a reliable knowledge of the world and a hopeful participation in it. In his doctoral dissertation Rahner had radically reinterpreted Thomas in light of transcendental philosophy, arriving at an understanding of the human person as a free being (a transcendental subject) who is structurally open to the self-communication of God, not in the explicit sense of receiving a direct vision or inspiration but through the mediations of ordinary human existence itself: family, culture, church, and especially the symbols that make these realities cohere. God's self-communication, freely offered and freely accepted through these mediations, is another way of describing what the tradition calls

---

Modernity: An Essay in the Hermeneutics of Nature and Culture (New Haven: Yale University Press, 1993). See also the work of Michel Foucault (e.g., *The Archeology of Knowledge* [New York: Pantheon, 1972]), who maps the discontinuities of culture in his "archaeological" projects and scrutinizes the notion of unbroken development of ideas, institutions, cultural forms, etc. For a discussion of these ideas in relation to the pluralism within the church, see Owen C. Thomas, "On Stepping Twice into the Same Church: Essence, Development, and Pluralism," *Anglican Theological Review* 70 (1988): 293–306.

grace. Rahner applied this transcendental framework to other dimensions of the faith tradition, including dogma.

Rahner's approach to dogma, and to its development, was the first systematic attempt to address the fact that dogma emerges within and is taught to a "world church" of a pluralism of faith experiences that cannot be neatly contained under the rubric of organic development. While his treatment of dogma takes into account Newman's concern for the organic development of dogma from the unchanging substance of faith, it also takes into account the pluralism of faith experiences within the church from which dogma emerges and the ongoing interpretation of that experience as constitutive of the tradition of faith that unifies the entire church. Within a transcendental framework, Rahner understood dogma to be not only propositional teaching but more fundamentally a symbol mediating the ongoing self-communication of God to the church as a whole—a symbol drawing the church, in all its pluralism, into a unity.

Like Newman, Rahner held that revelation transmits more than intellectual truth. Whereas Newman likened revelation to the impression of an idea—a divine idea—upon the mind of the church, Rahner held that revelation was primarily the history of the transcendental contact between God and humanity. Revelation belongs to the order of human events and the human experience of God in history as much as to the order of intellectual truth propositionally stated. Thus, the dogmatic statement "must not be mistaken for the thing itself, i.e., the event of revelation, or respectively must not be confused with a statement which can be made only by starting from the thing itself."[3] Like Newman, Rahner held that dogmatic statements are indispensable. Yet like Newman, he also held that a purely propositional approach to truth can ignore the fact that language is inherently limited in its capacity to express sufficiently,

---

[3] Karl Rahner, "What Is a Dogmatic Statement?" in *Theological Investigations*, vol. 5, trans. Karl-H. Kruger (Baltimore: Helicon, 1966), 54. In the notes below, the page of the English translation is followed in parentheses by the German reference in those cases where an emendation or new translation has been made. In this case, we have consulted "Was ist eine dogmatische Aussage?" in *Schriften zur Theologie*, Band 5 (Zurich: Benziger, 1962), 68.

much less exhaustively, the full meaning of revelation. "The reality referred to by theological statements is of an immeasurable richness and infinite fullness. [B]ut the terminological material available for characterizing this reality is extremely limited. . . . Such a limited terminology can never be adequate for what is meant."[4] Rather, an adequate understanding of dogma must begin "with the thing itself"—that which dogma expresses—the living contact between God and the pluriform reality of the church. But we can approach "the thing itself" only through the filters of human experience. Rahner therefore began his treatment of dogma with a consideration of faith experience, ultimately with what he called the "faith consciousness" of the entire church, the church's "view into the infinite fullness of what is meant by faith."[5] He rooted dogma in faith experience itself and developed a notion of dogma as a symbolic expression of faith that is not necessarily only propositional, one that allows a wider understanding of dogma as confessional by nature.

In order to arrive at this position, he extrapolated from his earlier work on the transcendental experience of faith, which focused on the transcendental structures of an individual person, to the transcendental experience of the entire church. Faith begins with revelation, what God discloses of God's very self to human beings in natural and supernatural ways. If the transcendental experience of faith could be reckoned as an ecclesial experience, not only as a purely subjective experience, then dogma could be understood as a symbolic mediation of God's self-communication to the searching consciousness of the entire church, in all its pluralism. But in order to appreciate how Rahner did this, we first need to focus more closely on what he meant by "transcendental experience" and then consider how it applies to the church as a whole.

---

[4] Ibid.

[5] Rahner, "What Is a Dogmatic Statement?" 54 (German, 68). Strictly speaking, "a statement which can be made only by starting from the thing itself" is a kerygmatic statement, such as Peter's confession of faith in Jesus as the Christ. Subsequent dogmatic or confessional statements rest upon layers of the historical experience of faith through which such kerygmatic statements are mediated. For Rahner, it would thus be impossible to conceive of an authentically kerygmatic statement made subsequent to the closure of categorical revelation at the end of the apostolic generation.

THE TRANSCENDENTAL EXPERIENCE OF FAITH

The dogmatic tradition of the church strives to bring to expression the "infinite fullness" of faith experience. This "faith experience" of the church is based on what Rahner describes as the "transcendental experience" of God. Rahner defined transcendental experience as "the subjective, unthematic, necessary and unfailing consciousness of the knowing subject that is co-present in every spiritual act of knowledge, and the subject's openness to the unlimited expanse of all possible reality."[6] An entire theological understanding of the human person is packed into this pithy definition, a theological anthropology for the individual spiritual subject, which Rahner extended by analogy to the entire church as an intersubjective community of faith.

Genuine development of the dogmatic dimension of the faith tradition guarantees the constant self-identity of the self-communication of God, the *revelatum*. The traditional issue of immutability raised by Vincent of Lerins and addressed by Newman is transposed by Rahner from the constancy of a divinely impressed "idea" to the constant self-identity of the *revelatum* always offered to the church as God's self-communication in grace. That which God once communicated to the apostolic generation continues to be communicated to the "transcendental subjectivity" of the whole church through numerous and continuing historical mediations. Authentic dogmatic development does not deny that this transcendental self-communication of God is perennially self-identical, despite the fact that, as a result of its explication in the faith consciousness of the church, it becomes more explicitly known.

How did Rahner accomplish this move from the individual spiritual subject to the spiritual subjectivity of the whole church? We will examine here three steps in that move: (1) an elaboration of the notion of person as spiritual subject, (2) an explanation of how the "real symbol" mediates transcendental experience, and (3) a specification of the relationship between language and the *inter*subjective nature of transcendental experience.

---

[6] Karl Rahner, *Foundations of Christian Faith: An Introduction to the Idea of Christianity*, trans. William V. Dych (New York: Seabury, 1978), 20.

The Person as Spiritual Subject

First, Rahner saw the human person as the "event" of God's self-communication. The human subject is fashioned by grace and "built" as a potential hearer of God's word. The relationship between God and the human creature is one of formal cause to effect: God, the absolutely transcendent goal of the movements of human transcendence, is also the innermost cause of the movements of self-transcendence. The human person is thus drawn "supernaturally" from the beginning of one's personal existence toward transcendence. When I experience the joy of learning more about something that really interests me, or move out of myself into the risk of love, I am moving toward the goal that at the same time draws and impels me. In this view, all knowing and loving have their source and finality in God.

The possibility of a living contact with God is given "pre-reflexively." This implies that we are not always explicitly aware of our openness to God as source and goal of our lives. Our openness to God is given with the ordinary experiences of human consciousness as it is mediated in daily life. A pre-reflexive awareness is more akin to an atmosphere, to the air that we breathe, than to any discrete knowledge content. A baby has a pre-reflexive awareness of the love of its parents, even though the infant cannot conceptualize or articulate it. Rahner's point is that we are pre-reflexively open to all that is, and ultimately to God. This openness is the precondition for all knowledge. Knowledge of something other than ourselves, or even of ourselves, is not exhausted by objective descriptions or by possession of an objective datum.

When we listen to a word spoken to us, not only do we hear the audible sounds and take stock of their content but, in a posture of anticipatory openness, we allow ourselves to receive the word in its fullness, to be imbued with its meaning. What is communicated has a way of shaping how we hear it and what we hear. In this sense, our knowing is a "receptive" knowing. Rahner elaborates:

> That is to say, one is not antecedently in possession of his knowledge in virtue of his nature, but has such knowledge only inasmuch as an object displays itself to him of its own accord. . . . And so, when one turns towards something outside oneself desiring to know it, one does not assume control over a cognition that is already completely established within one's own essence. . . . If, then, human knowledge

is essentially receptive knowledge, the basic structure of knowledge of the thing initially received and the way it is received will persist throughout all subsequent acts of knowledge and determine the structure of human knowledge in general.[7]

Correlatively, the knowledge that pertains to faith is not simply possessed by a knowing subject; faith knowledge is rather the divine self-communication as it is received by the ontologically open human subject, a person who is a potential "hearer" of a message or recipient of a communication.[8] This philosophical analysis of human knowing is the presupposition for Rahner's later demonstration of a continuity in transcendental faith consciousness from the apostolic generation to the present time. The entire church is and always has been a "hearer" of God's word.

While the knowing that is proper to transcendental experience is "receptive" knowing, knowing also has an active dimension. The knowing subject at the same time always moves ahead of what is known thematically, in what Rahner describes as an "unthematic" pre-apprehension of it. When I enter into the world of a Hitchcock movie such as *Vertigo*, I do not coolly analyze the movie as I watch it, breaking it down into discrete bits of analyzable data, scene by scene; I allow the entire world of the film (San Francisco in the 1950s) to become my world, and I give myself over to it. In doing so, I anticipate as I watch the movie the unfolding of the lives (of the characters played by Jimmy Stewart and Kim Novak) that takes place before my eyes. I wonder about what will unfold next on the screen, whether Jimmy Stewart will in the end rescue Kim Novak. Or when I read a Jane Austen novel thick with plot and characterization, I move not only with but ahead of the characters in anticipating possible intrigues and outcomes. I am silently present before the action, even within it, in a mode of anticipatory participation, even before I know how the plot will unfold. So too with the transcendental experience of God. My ontological openness includes a movement in pre-apprehension of what is being communicated to me, even if it is largely unnamed. I enter actively into the experi-

---

[7] Karl Rahner, *Hearers of the Word*, trans. Michael Richards (New York: Herder & Herder, 1969), 119–20; originally published as *Hörer des Wortes: Zur Grundlegung einer Religionsphilosophie*, ed. J. Metz (Munich: Kösel, 1963), 147–48.

[8] Rahner, *Hearers of the Word*, 22 (German, 37).

ence, giving myself over to it through the largely unreflected moments of my own human existence, projecting myself ahead of myself.

This transcendental relation between God and the human person who "hears" God's communication opens up the meaning of human life itself. There is a divine self-communication to the open human subject; the human subject receives the communication and responds to it with active curiosity and wonder. A back-and-forth movement between the human "question" and the "answer" of divine self-communication results in growing knowledge not only of the terminus of this transcendental experience, God, but also of oneself. As Rahner puts it:

> Every answer is always just the beginning of a new question. Human beings experience themselves as infinite possibility because in practice and in theory they necessarily place every sought-after result in question. . . . They are the question which rises up before themselves, empty, but really and inescapably, and which can never be settled and never adequately answered by themselves.[9]

In and through this movement of question and answer between God and human beings, we transcend ourselves, moving into a deeper knowledge both of ourselves as spirit and of God as mystery.

Historical Mediation through the Real Symbol

The second element in Rahner's move to the spiritual subjectivity of the church is the complementary relationship between transcendental subjectivity and its historical mediation. Rahner's method assumes complementary poles: one beginning from the standpoint of transcendental subjectivity, the other from the standpoint of the data of historical experience. Transcendental experience becomes an object of reflexive knowledge as it is lived within history. The events of history themselves and the testimony of human witnesses constitute the history of salvation, but only from the standpoint of transcendental subjectivity. Virtually all of Rahner's theological analysis takes into account these transcendental and categorical coordinates. For example, his use of the term "word of God" can be

[9] Rahner, *Foundations of Christian Faith,* 32 (translation emended).

construed in both transcendental and categorical senses. In the transcendental sense, the word of God is identical with the revealing Logos, the self-utterance of God and his self-communication through history. This revealing Logos becomes incarnate in Christ. The categorical sense begins with the incarnate Logos in Christ and includes the *kerygma* (proclamation of the gospel of salvation), which, in the person of Christ and in the mission of his apostles, announces the divine message of salvation uttered in Christ. This *kerygma* is, in turn, mediated by the categorical word of God in scripture.

Both the transcendental and the categorical coordinates are inalienable elements of a comprehensive understanding of faith. Without the categorical coordinate, we risk abstracting faith from the concrete conditions of history and culture. Without the transcendental coordinate, we risk reducing theological investigation to a mere "a posteriori gathering of random facts" arranged to buttress a dogmatic position.[10] There can be no transcendental experience that is not also and essentially an experience that takes place within space and time, that is, within history.

Now this historical mediation comes to expression. Since a direct, unmediated presentation of God to the human subject is impossible, the transcendental relation requires a human word, "a vicarious sign of one who is not given in himself."[11] Here Rahner introduces the notion of "real symbol." A real symbol is the "highest and most primordial manner in which one reality represents another . . . [hence] the highest and most primordial representation in which a reality renders another present (first for itself and then for the other), and allows it 'to be there.'"[12] All transcendental experience moves toward expression, and the real symbol is the means by which the reality of that experience becomes fully realized. Just as there could be no eucharist without the symbolic mediation of it

[10] See Leo J. O'Donovan, S.J., "Orthopraxis and Theological Method in Karl Rahner," *Proceedings of the Catholic Theological Society of America* 35 (1980): 48-51.

[11] Rahner, *Hearers of the Word*, 114 (German, 141).

[12] Karl Rahner, "The Theology of Symbol," in *Theological Investigations*, vol. 4, trans. Kevin Smyth (Baltimore: Helicon, 1966), 225; originally published as "Zur Theologie des Symbols," in *Schriften zur Theologie*, Band 4 (Zurich: Benziger, 1961), 279.

through word, bread, and wine, so there can be no transcendental experience of God that does not actually realize itself through some sort of symbolic mediation.

A real symbol functions with a transcendental-categorical framework. As William Dych explains it:

> To express . . . the polarity or the dialectic between these two equally necessary and equally primary poles in human existence, the transcendental and the historical, Rahner develops the category of symbol, or more precisely, real symbol. It is of the very nature of human existence to express itself in order to be itself, and in this expression or symbol the symbolized becomes fully real. Hence the universal, transcendental possibility of salvation must become actual by coming to expression in concrete, particular histories of salvation, and the universal, transcendental possibility of revelation must become actual by coming to expression in concrete, particular revelations.[13]

The church itself is the "symbolic embodiment of the Spirit of God and of the inner history of the dialogue between God's free love and human freedom."[14] A dogmatic statement in the formal sense of a creed or formal definition of faith is thus a linguistic symbol of the transcendental relation between the hearing church and the word spoken to it. It expresses the self-communication of God as that communication is received or "heard" by the church at particular points in history. Although this self-communication is expressed in human language, it remains God's word. The dogmatic symbol not only allows a living contact between God and humanity to assume a specifiable content that is really present in the faith consciousness of the church, but it is also one of the principal forms in which the revealed word is announced to and confessed by the church itself.

Linguisticality and Intersubjectivity

If a real symbol really expresses the reality it presents, then it is in some sense a form of language. The history of the transcendental

---

[13] William V. Dych, "Theology in a New Key," in *A World of Grace: An Introduction to the Themes and Foundations of Karl Rahner's Theology*, ed. Leo O'Donovan (New York: Seabury, 1980), 14–15.

[14] Rahner, "Theology of Symbol," 243 (German, 330–31).

relation between the hearer of the word and the word itself is actualized in language. By language we do not mean here only written and verbal propositions, but also other forms of symbolic communication, such as liturgical ritual, music, and poetry. All of these are modes of human expression that could potentially function as forms of symbolic mediation.

Transcendental experience, therefore, has a "linguistic" characteristic. This "linguisticality" of transcendental experience does not mean that language is merely a device to translate transcendental experience into speech. Rather, language derives from the transcendental nature of the human subject, a nature that is realized through what Heidegger described as the human tendency toward "discourse" (*Rede*), that is, the structural orientation of human beings toward self-communication. Discourse (*Rede*) is thus the ontological foundation of language (*Sprache*) in the ordinary sense of the term. Discourse is the human person's way of disclosing oneself to the world of other human subjects through communication by bringing into actual words the transcendental experience that is itself already linguistic, by nature constituted by an orientation toward communication.[15] In Rahner's thought, language is the means by which a person reaches a reflexive self-knowledge.

> We observe that original, non-propositional, unreflexive yet knowing possession of a reality on the one hand, and reflexive (propositional) articulated consciousness of this original knowing on the other, are not competing opposites but reciprocally interacting factors of a single experience that necessarily has a history. Simple basic knowing would grow dim if, because it is richer and fuller, it would refuse to allow itself to grow out into a reflexive knowing involving ideas and propositions.[16]

Human self-possession therefore comes "in formula. A reflexive or formulated self-understanding is itself an important moment in the

[15] Martin Heidegger, *Being and Time*, trans. John Macquarrie and Edward Robinson (New York: Harper & Row, 1962), 203–10. "The existential-ontological foundation of language is discourse or talk. . . . The way discourse gets expressed is language."

[16] Karl Rahner, "The Development of Dogma," in *Theological Investigations*, vol. 1, trans. Cornelius Ernst (Baltimore: Helicon, 1961), 64–65; originally published as "Zur Frage der Dogmenentwicklung," in *Schriften zur Theologie*, Band 1 (Zurich: Benziger, 1962), 77.

whole of personal self-possession."[17] I know, I know that I know, and I articulate my self-knowing. There is no way we can come to a knowledge of ourselves apart from the symbolic mediation of that knowledge in language. This linguistic possession of self in the act of knowing allows for the disclosing of what is known, expressing it in a form that captures it in the symbolism of language.

Because language is the medium of communication, the relation between the transcendental subject and the object of knowledge becomes in language the common property of a community of subjects. In an "intersubjective" community of transcendental subjects such as the church, no one's subjectivity can be adequately comprehended apart from the subjectivity of every other person. This is what makes a community a community, the exquisite balance between my own uniqueness and freedom and my dependence on and responsibility toward others for that uniqueness and freedom. For I am a unique person only in relation to and with other unique persons. Another person is not simply an object to me; I depend on that other person for my own awareness, for the possibility of even articulating my own experience. I learn that while my own experience is irreducibly personal, it is not so unique as to be incommunicable. The fact that I can and do communicate it, and receive the communication of others, rests upon and demonstrates the intersubjective nature of human community, including the community of the church.

In the intersubjective community of faith called the church, people communicate with one another in what could be called the dialogue of faith, as they pose questions to themselves, and sometimes to others, about the meaning of faith itself. This dialogue leads to a common lexicon and to common formulations of knowledge, meaning, and truth, as we see in the creeds. Indeed, "the common formula, the 'confession of a society,' which sustains that society, is a necessary goal to be pursued in the conversation that concerns the common search for truth."[18]

---

[17] Vincent Branick, *An Ontology of Understanding: Karl Rahner's Metaphysics of Knowledge in the Context of Modern German Hermeneutics*, Diss., Fribourg, 1971 (St. Louis: Marianist, 1971), 190.

[18] Karl Rahner, "A Small Fragment 'On the Collective Finding of Truth,'" in *Theological Investigations*, vol. 6, trans. Karl-H. and Boniface

These three principles: the human person as spiritual subject, the historical and symbolic mediation of transcendental experience, and the linguisticality of intersubjective experience, undergird Rahner's approach to dogma as a mediating symbol of faith for a world church. While Rahner's theology was built upon the model of individual spiritual subjectivity, these principles apply analogously to the intersubjective world of spiritual persons who constitute the spiritual subjectivity church, a community that comes to expression in and through the symbolic mediations of historical languages. Now we ask how dogma might function as an instrument of unity in such a world church, first by examining dogma's development within a transcendental framework, and then by viewing it in relation to the entire church's search for truth.

DOGMA IN A TRANSCENDENTAL FRAMEWORK

Rahner's treatment of dogma was almost exclusively linguistic, and more specifically propositional. He had in mind both the ordinary and the extraordinary teaching of the church. But he presented the notion of dogma within the context of transcendental experience, and more specifically, as a functioning symbol of the experience of God. The dogmatic proposition, therefore, stands as the primary instance, the prime analogue, of a wider understanding of dogma not only as teaching but as confession of faith in liturgy, church practices, and traditions. As we have seen, Rahner understood this faith as a transcendental relationship between the self-communication of the mystery of God and the world of human persons in relation to one another, an intersubjective community of faith. Thus, dogma is subject to a variety of modes of expression, but Rahner treated these with primary reference to the dogmatic statement as such. This raised for his critics some serious questions about the proper ordering of language to experience. On the resolution of this question Rahner's own approach to dogma would either stand or fall. Let us take a closer look at this question, beginning with Rahner's notion of revelation and its mediation in dogma.

Kruger (New York: Seabury, 1974), 84; originally published as "Kleines Fragment 'Über die kollektive Findung der Wahrheit,'" in *Schriften zur Theologie*, Band 6 (Zurich: Benziger, 1968), 106–7.

Revelation and Its Dogmatic Mediation

Rahner held that the dogmatic statement must be seen in relation to the self-communication of God to the human persons who as spiritual subjects receive this communication as grace, and to the historical actualization of this transcendental relation between God and humanity which revelation constitutes and which the church in particular receives. He saw revelation not only as historical events but more broadly as the "history of the transcendental relation between humans and God which is constituted by God's self-communication."[19] Revelation, then, includes (1) the transcendental communication and reception of God's grace; (2) the historical or categorical mediation of that grace in particular human ways, including the forms of religion; (3) the privileged self-disclosure of God in the person of Jesus Christ. The transcendental communication of God and the human reception of it are achieved ultimately in the specific categorical revelation of God in the historical person of Jesus Christ:

> God is revealed as communicating himself in absolute and merciful presence as God, that is, as the absolute mystery. The historical mediation of this transcendental experience is also revealed as valid, as bringing about and authenticating the absolute experience of God. The unique and final culmination of this history of revelation has already occurred and has revealed the absolute and irrevocable unity of God's transcendental self-communication to mankind and of its historical mediation in the one God-man Jesus Christ, who is at once God himself as communicated, the human acceptance of this communication and the final historical manifestation of this offer and acceptance.[20]

The historical deeds and words that mediate and convey revelation exist in a relation of mutual dependence. Scripture and tradition are not two separate and independent sources of revelation; they are rather two aspects of the human expression of the self-communication or "word" of God.[21] The word of revelation is truth

[19] Karl Rahner, "Revelation," in *Sacramentum Mundi* (New York: Herder & Herder, 1970), 5:348.

[20] Ibid., 349.

[21] Karl Rahner, "Scripture and Tradition," in *Theological Investigations*, vol. 6, trans. Karl-H. and Boniface Kruger (New York: Seabury, 1974),

because it is the communication of God himself; as a human word it expresses the content of this communication through the various historically conditioned ways the church has received this communication. As a human word, therefore, dogma mediates and expresses the transcendental relation between God and the world of human intersubjectivity that constitutes the spiritual subjectivity of the church. Thus, the transcendental experience of God is the way God's "truth" is communicated to, received, and expressed by the church as a whole.

Rahner's notion of truth here reflects both Heidegger and scholasticism. Heidegger rejected the correspondence theory of truth, by which we mean that a proposition must "agree" with the perception of a thing:

> Truth is not the mark of some correct proposition made by a human "subject" in respect of an "object" and which then—in precisely what sphere we do not know—counts as "true"; truth is rather the revelation of what is, a revelation through which something "overt" comes into force.[22]

The essence of truth is the free openness of the transcendental subject to all that is, so that in the act of knowing, being is allowed to appear.[23] Rahner adopted this Heideggerian way of thinking to the extent that the truth of revelation is not merely a propositional

---

98–112. Rahner elaborates in *Foundations of Christian Faith*, 377–78: "Scripture itself is the concrete process and the objectification of the original church's consciousness of faith, and by means of it this consciousness of faith is 'transmitted' to later ages of the church. The formation of the canon is a process whose legitimacy cannot be established by scripture alone, but rather it is itself a fundamental moment in the tradition." See also Second Vatican Council, *Dei verbum*, 9: "Hence sacred tradition and scripture are bound together in a close and reciprocal relationship. They both flow from the same divine well-spring, merge together to some extent, and are on course towards the same end." *Decrees of the Ecumenical Councils*, 2:974 (DS 4212).

[22] Martin Heidegger, "On the Essence of Truth," in *Existence and Being*, trans. R. F. C. Hull and Alan Crick (Chicago: Henry Regnery, 1949), 309.

[23] See William Reiser's treatment of Heidegger's notion of truth in "An Essay on the Development of Dogma in a Heideggerian Context: A Non-Theological Explanation of Theological Heresy," *The Thomist* 30 (1975): 471–95.

datum approximating an experience of God, but is rather the divinely initiated transcendental experience itself in which God's self-communication to the human subject is freely received and heard. In this transcendental experience of God, God "sends forth this truth . . . as a free disclosure of his own nature and will."[24]

Unlike Heidegger, however, Rahner did not reject the traditional understanding of the scholastic notion of truth. The propositions that mediate this truth and attempt to express it "are an '*adequatio intellectus et rei*' [an adequation between the mind and the objective reality] in so far as they state absolutely nothing that is false." But he adds a caveat: "Anyone who proposes to regard these propositions of faith, because they are wholly true, as in themselves *adequate* to the matter in question, i.e. as exhaustive statements, would be falsely elevating human truth to God's simple and exhaustive knowledge of himself and of all that takes its origin from him."[25]

While revelation communicates truth, then, this is no abstract truth; it is the knowledge of God that emerges from the transcendental relation initiated by God that becomes historical in Jesus Christ. Still, the transcendental experience of God, and the truth it communicates, ultimately in the person of Jesus Christ, cannot be known apart from its various categorical mediations, one of which is dogma. While this truth about God revealed in Jesus is partly expressed in linguistic and historical symbols (scripture, creeds, ordinary teachings, liturgical formulas, etc.), the truth known in the transcendental relation with God cannot be made fully equivalent to propositional truth, for it is essentially personal, revealed in the person of Christ.

Lindbeck's Critique of Rahner's Approach

Lutheran theologian George Lindbeck has criticized Rahner's treatment of the transcendental experience of faith for confusing the order of language and faith experience. Religious experience, Lindbeck argues, depends on a socially contextualized doctrinal language; doctrinal language does not emerge from an as yet

---

[24] Karl Rahner, "On Heresy," in *Inquiries*, trans. W. J. O'Hara (New York: Herder & Herder, 1964), 404.

[25] Rahner, "Development of Dogma," 44 (German, 54).

unfocused religious experience. Lindbeck targets the transcendental Thomists, notably B. Lonergan and Rahner, but includes with
them F. Schleiermacher, R. Otto, M. Eliade, and others in a common criticism:

> [W]hatever the variations, thinkers of this tradition all locate ulti-
> mately significant contact with whatever is finally important to reli-
> gion in the prereflective experiential depths of the self and regard
> the public or outer features of religion as expressive and evocative
> objectifications (i.e., nondiscursive symbols) of internal experi-
> ence.[26]

In Lindbeck's view, systems such as Rahner's confuse the proper
ordering of the inner and the outer. They would begin with an
inner experience which "cannot be expressed except in public and
intersubjective forms." This inner experience, furthermore, is
somewhat mystified in a way that "is more than doubtful."[27] Such
"experiential-expressivist" approaches fail to see that "[i]nstead of
deriving external features of a religion from inner experience, it is
the inner experiences which are viewed as derivative."[28] They are
derivative, to be specific, from the language of religion, which functions primarily neither as propositional truth nor as expression of
inner experience, but "in the story it tells and in the grammar that
informs the way the story is told and used."[29] The origin of and
change in doctrine, like other forms of religious language, "must be
understood, not as proceeding from new experiences, but as resulting from the interactions of a cultural-linguistic system with changing situations."[30]

Rahner held that doctrine, i.e., the dogmatic statement, is indeed
a linguistic symbol of what God discloses and of what human beings
in the church experience of God. But contrary to Lindbeck's reading, a dogmatic statement, as a symbol of the church's reception of
the truth communicated to it in Christ, is not merely a verbal objectification of the content of faith.[31] Because it is a confession of faith,
it renders present both the revealed "content" of faith and the

[26] Lindbeck, *Nature of Doctrine*, 21.
[27] Ibid., 38.
[28] Ibid., 32.
[29] Ibid., 80.
[30] Ibid., 39.
[31] Rahner, "What Is a Dogmatic Statement?" 48 (German, 61).

church's act of faith.[32] The relationship between experience and language in Rahner's thought is not simply a correlation between the outward expression of some inner event and the inner event itself. Although dogmatic statements function as one specification of the linguisticality of the transcendental experience of faith, the experience always exceeds the verbal expression. At the same time, the verbal expression informs the experience. Faith is necessarily verbally mediated. While the truth of faith is known before it becomes the explicit object of intellectual knowledge, it cannot be understood as a pre-reflexive experience or unthematic knowledge apart from an articulation of it in reflexive faith consciousness. This ordering of experience and language is rooted in Thomas Aquinas's ordering of the knowledge of faith and the articulation of it. The articulation takes place in a thorough knowledge of that which is being articulated; the articulation is essential to the knowledge of it. However, the act of faith does not finally terminate with the articulation of it, but tends toward the "thing itself" of faith, that is, toward that which is the source and goal of the knowledge of faith, the divine mystery revealed in the person of Christ.[33]

The Limits of Dogmatic Language

As we have noted, language cannot possibly express all that is experienced and known in revelation, yet revelation must necessarily be expressed symbolically. As symbols, dogmatic statements are in a sense identical with the truth of revelation because they "share in its characteristic as the word of God."[34] They thus operate as symbols in the richest sense of the word: not as mere signs but as linguistic embodiments of that which they represent. The ancient "symbol" or Creed of Nicaea, for example, is valuable not only because it reflects in language the perennial belief of the church but also because it functions as a symbolic embodiment of the truth of faith it conveys.

While dogmatic statements symbolize the church's living contact

---

[32] Ibid., 51 (German, 64).

[33] See *Summa theologiae*, 2-2, 1, 2, resp. and ad 2.

[34] Karl Rahner, "Theology in the New Testament," in *Theological Investigations*, vol. 5, trans. Karl-H. Kruger (Baltimore: Helicon, 1966), 26.

with God, this is a living contact that assumes a variety of modalities in different historical and cultural settings. Although a particular proposition "can be obligatory" or binding, or at least "must be taken into account in any interpretation of the declarations made by the Church," a dogma is nevertheless essentially a provisional and proleptic statement.[35] It is provisional because it in fact is not "the thing itself"; it is human speech that can be surpassed by a more apt language. It is proleptic because it directs the mind of faith toward a knowledge of God that is not yet fully attained and cannot be contained within propositional language alone. This is true even of the creeds and of formally defined dogmas of faith. The fullness of revealed truth can only be expressed proleptically in successive historical and cultural mediations of it in creeds, liturgical formulations, and of course, dogmatic statements. We could well draw a circle between the ongoing transcendental experience of God, that which is not explicitly thematized, and the ever-deepening articulation of it. Rahner described how this circular relationship between faith experience and its articulation obtained even at the very outset of Christian faith in the original experience of the person of Jesus in the apostolic church:

> Even in the many cases where our Lord's spoken word as such is the necessary starting-point of the Apostles' faith because the actual content of Revelation is available in no other way, these words are heard in the context of a vivid experience of daily life in his company. And so, even in these cases, the concrete experience is an essential presupposition for the true and ever deepening understanding of the words spoken and heard. These sayings are not in themselves explicit enough; rather they require the complete experience, which in turn becomes continually more explicit and reflexively intelligible as the content of these sayings is unfolded.[36]

Thus, the creative tension between the transcendental experience of revelation and the mediation of it does not entirely disappear in

[35] Rahner, "What Is a Dogmatic Statement?" 54 (German, 68).

[36] Rahner, "Development of Dogma," 66 (German, 78). Robert L. Richard explains: "Experience in turn is realized through actually stating what it knows. In this way, reflection illuminates experience, and becomes a natural intrinsic factor in its continued existence." See "Rahner's Theory of Doctrinal Development," *Proceedings of the Catholic Theological Society of America* 18 (1963): 171.

the dogmatic statement itself. While dogma emerges as a symbolic mediation of revelation that really expresses the "truth" of the transcendental experience of revelation, it remains human mediation. Like scripture itself, dogmatic statements are spoken from within a particular historical situation. A dogmatic statement of the church shares the laws and structures of ordinary statements. It expresses the intention or claim of the speaker and establishes a definite objective content which presumably can be understood by those who listen. Like ordinary statements, the dogmatic statement depends on the capacity of a given language to express an intended meaning through dependence on metaphor and analogy.[37] Consequently, like many ordinary statements, the dogmatic statement is marked by a tension between what is said and what is meant. This tension is perhaps greater in dogmatic statements than in most ordinary statements, for the dogmatic statement refers to an experience that lies "beyond sense experience."[38] To put it differently, in the case of formal dogma, the immediate speaker is the church, but the word uttered is not simply its own. Hence, it cannot express all that it intends to communicate nor all that is communicated in revelation to the faith consciousness of the church.[39]

THE COLLECTIVE SEARCH FOR TRUTH

As we have seen, the self-explication of the meaning of revelation in the mind of the church involves the transcendental experience of the church in its living contact with God and the historical expression of this experience in dogmatic statements and other forms of dogmatic expression. How, then, does Rahner understand the

[37] Rahner, "What Is a Dogmatic Statement?" 46.

[38] Ibid., 47 (German, 60).

[39] See Rahner, "Development of Dogma," 67 (German, 79): "The explicit proposition is at the same time more and less than its implicit source. More, because as reflexively formulated it elucidates the original, spiritually simple possession of the reality and in this way enriches it. Less, because it never does more than express reflexively a part of what is already possessed spiritually."

"whole church" to function in its articulation of faith through dogmatic teaching and confession? Simply put, the church of a particular time and place "hears" the word of revelation through particular historical mediations and inquires into its meaning. For example, liberation theologians in Latin America have inquired into the meaning of the saving work of Christ revealed in scripture and tradition. A questioning of the revealed word takes place not only through formal theology but more often in the largely unarticulated living of faith that takes place as people search, for example, through liturgy and the practice of faith in real life, for the "co-communicated" content or meaning of their experience of God in the grace of revelation. Gradually, this co-communicated content of the grace of revelation is "discovered," and its virtualities for the people of faith of a particular time and place become clearer.[40]

This searching for and discovery of the co-communicated content of revelation take on the "dialectical" form of a conversation, moving back and forth between what has been "said" in revelation and what has been "heard" by the church, and result in the possibility of new dogmatic expressions of teaching and confession of faith. Because this dialectic between hearing and questioning the word of revelation involves an inquiry into the confessional statements of the church, Rahner's approach does not abandon strict scholarly attention "to what has been said in original revelation." This includes

> strict concern for the meaning of what has been heard, making use of all the methods at the disposal of a liberal and human discipline (philology, history, logic, etc.); comparison and connection of the propositions so heard and understood (*analogia fidei*); inquiry into the logical consequences resulting from these operations (deductions), etc.[41]

However, the possibility of an authentic dogmatic expression for the whole church rests in the relation between what is received and the recipient church's mode of knowing it, not only in these specific methods of inquiry. The faith consciousness of the church contains not only what the church can explicitly conceptualize and articulate in dogmatic teachings but all that is co-communicated to it in non-

[40] Rahner, "Development of Dogma," 73 (German, 86).
[41] Ibid., 74 (German, 86–87).

conceptual and nonpropositional form and expressed as confession. The church moves from the stage where it possesses a truth without consciously recognizing it as revealed by God to the stage of making such an assertion through teaching and confession of faith in a variety of particular times and places.

Just as the transcendental subject moves toward a full intellectual penetration of the truth he or she has accepted as his or her own, so too does the "believing mind of the Church" in and through the particular faith consciousness of the various local churches. Dogma as symbol does not function in abstraction from this subjective participation of the whole church through the particular churches in the act of faith. To the contrary, it is only as the church lives its faith within concrete history that it inquires into the fullness of the truth of revelation and that the co-communicated message emerges. As the faith consciousness of parts of the church becomes clearer, through ongoing dialogue among the various local churches and voices present within the church, the possibility of a catholic consensus becomes more promising. Let us now examine more closely this dimension of Rahner's approach to dogma.

Dogma and the Mind of the Whole Church

Dogma functions within the mind of the whole church and not merely within the minds of certain individuals within it. By the "mind of the church" Rahner meant neither the views of hierarchical teachers alone nor the scientifically measured opinion of the faithful on any given issue, but rather the *sensus fidelium* of the whole ecclesiastical communion, which can itself become the object of explicit reflection. Rahner echoed Newman when he argued that before dogmatic definitions are made by the hierarchical magisterium, "the whole Church probably already believes clearly enough the doctrine about to be defined" and that this fact "is probably even the justification of the contents of the definition." This position does not deny the rightful exercise of the hierarchical magisterium. Nor does it imply that prior to a definition "every individual member already explicitly believes the given definition in question as already revealed by God. It only means that this faith already found in the Church is considered to belong to the collective moral subjectivity of the Church."[42]

In dogmatic definitions by a pope or a council, the faith consciousness of the entire church "attains effective self-awareness, in a manner which is authoritative for the individual members of the Church."[43] The magisterium plays a key role in the interpretation of that which is being communicated to the church through history and in particular historical moments. This is evident, for example, in the interpretation of scripture:

> Basically the Catholic church maintains that the community of believers can give at least a basic interpretation of scripture which is binding on individual Christians. It does this in its common profession of faith and with the help of the organs which form the common consciousness of those who profess the same faith. Otherwise, of course, the church basically ceases to exist as a reality which is independent of one's own subjectivity and private theology.[44]

But the church as a whole, and not only isolated individuals within it (including the teachers within the church), comes to a reflexive awareness of the truth which it already possesses:

> For in the Church there must be a common faith, a common confession, and a praise of God for his grace in a tongue which can be spoken by all. And this must always be done anew at each moment. Confronted with a common spiritual situation which, being common, must always be grasped and understood again in common the traditional message must always be grasped anew in common.[45]

Beyond a theology of individual belief, Rahner proposes a theology of the church where the common belief of the church has as its horizon the pluralism of the particular experiences of faith to be found in the world church. That which unites these experiences in a unity is not only the hierarchical church itself, but the transcen-

---

[42] Rahner, "Considerations on the Development of Dogma," in *Theological Investigations,* vol. 4, trans. Kevin Smyth (Baltimore: Helicon, 1966), 33; originally published as "Überlegung zur Dogmenentwicklung," in *Schriften zur Theologie,* Band 4 (Zurich: Benziger, 1961), 48.

[43] Ibid., 34 (German, 48–49).

[44] Rahner, *Foundations of Christian Faith,* 363–64.

[45] Rahner, "What Is a Dogmatic Statement?" 54 (German, 66).

dental experience of God which is common to all parts of the church, differently mediated.

The Common "Revelatum" and Ecclesial Consensus

If we assume that the experience of faith of the apostolic genera-tion (the transcendental relation between the church and God's self-communication) was substantially similar to that of succeeding generations, then we must also assume that the apostolic genera-tion handed on more than propositions. The apostolic generation passed on its living contact with the God of revelation, acquired through first-generation knowledge of Christ.[46] Rahner states:

> [The] "*successio apostolica*" [apostolic succession], in a full and com-prehensive sense, hands on to the post-apostolic church, and pre-cisely with respect to faith knowledge, not simply additions to a body of propositions, but living experience: . . . the very reality, then, of what they have experienced in Christ. Their own experience is pre-served and present together with their word. Spirit and word together form the lasting active possibility of an experience which is fundamentally the same as that of the apostles.[47]

The "truth" that the apostles were commissioned by Christ to pass on was the transcendental experience of God in revelation, the *rev-elatum*. The *revelatum* that was fully given and "closed" in a categor-ical sense with the death and resurrection of Jesus Christ and the experience of the apostolic generation is continually offered in a transcendental sense to those persons who constitute the church. Therefore, the authentic dogmatic expression of the truth of faith must correspond to that faith experience that remains in continuity with the faith experience of the apostles.

This means again that the dogmatic statement is not simply an expression of abstract truth; it is a symbol of faith as it is lived, both taught and confessed:

> A dogmatic statement, whenever it is genuine and realizes its true nature, is thus not merely an ordinary statement about some theo-

---

[46] Rahner, "What Is a Dogmatic Statement?" 171–72; idem, "Develop-ment of Dogma," 211. See *Dei verbum* 8, in *Decrees of the Ecumenical Coun-cils*, 2:974.

[47] Rahner, "Development of Dogma," 68 (German, 80).

logical object (about something to which the Christian faith itself refers originally), but is also in its very execution—in as much as it is the self-accomplishment of the subject—an exercise [*Vollzug*] of faith.[48]

Because it is an "exercise" of faith, dogma renders present both the revealed "content" of faith received by the church, and the church's act of faith in receiving, interpreting, and transmitting it: "In spite of all its conceptual reflection, it leads toward the historical event of salvation, rendering the event present by confessing that it is brought about by it. It does not merely speak 'about' this event but tries to bring people into a real relationship with it."[49] And because the exercise of faith is an ecclesial act, the dogmatic statement is an ecclesial expression of the church's confession of faith. The revealed message is always grasped anew by the church, and the dogmatic statement is the vehicle by which the entire church not only reaches a reflective grasp of the content of revelation but expresses what it grasps. As an ecclesial expression of faith, a confession, a particular dogmatic statement can only reflect a certain point in the dialogue of faith that takes place within the entire church as the self-communication of God in Jesus Christ is continually received, interpreted, and articulated. For this reason, Rahner allowed for the possibility of new creedal formulations. In the dogmatic statement, the catholic ideal of the universality of faith is drawn into a creative tension with particular inculturated experiences of faith.

As noted earlier, the dogmatic statement is for Rahner the prime analogue for dogma; it does not exhaust the category of dogma for the church. What is true of dogmatic statements is, *mutatis mutandis*, true of other forms of dogmatic expression, such as some liturgical, disciplinary, and theological traditions. These forms of dogmatic expression are also symbolic mediations of the history of the transcendental relation between God and humanity. And as we have also seen, the "content" of this transcendental experience unfolds in the faith consciousness of the church. Rahner explains:

> It must, of course, also be remembered that this mediation, being an historical one, is necessarily always social; it is "*ecclesia*'" in the deepest sense of the word. It therefore includes an acceptance of the

[48] Rahner, "What Is a Dogmatic Statement?" 48 (German, 61).
[49] Ibid., 51 (German, 64).

never totally explicit belief of the Church, the community of believers. That belief of the Church is always, whether in the Church or in the individual, a unity of sign and truth beyond [human] disposal and decision.[50]

Rahner continues: "Where the culmination and final form of God's eschatological self-communication and revelation in Christ is present explicitly and in a socially constituted form, we have what is called the Church. The Church receives and announces this absolute revelation."[51]

The intersubjective community of spiritual subjects who constitute the church receives, interprets, and articulates the content of this experience. As this truth unfolds in the faith consciousness of the church and becomes increasingly thematic, there follows a development of the propositional and other forms of dogmatic expression of this truth. But for Rahner, even more than for Newman, the unifying function of dogma will depend on the degree to which it can be shown that dogma expresses the faith of a church whose catholicity is realized by the consensus of many voices. This concern leads him to a practical consideration of the faith consciousness of the entire church in its collective search for truth.

Moving beyond Newman

Rahner held that just as the faith consciousness of the entire church is ontologically open to a living contact with God in history, so the dogmatic statement is, by virtue of its nature as a symbol of this living contact, open to explication within the mind of the church. But this occurs only as the church's faith consciousness "comes to itself" in a reflexive awareness of the truth that it possesses as a result of its living contact with God within and through the mediations of particular historical and cultural circumstances.

Rahner's description of this process is reminiscent of Newman's description of the development of an idea:

> The Church as a whole considers a thought which arises for her out of the whole content of its faith: it ripens and grows ever more bound up with the whole content of its faith as the Church lives [its

[50] Rahner, "Revelation," 353.
[51] Ibid.

faith] and realizes it. And so the Church of a certain day . . . finds itself simply there, believing in this special manner. . . . What interests us here is that the subject of this passage in the development of dogma from groping to grasping, from thinking to the assent of faith, is first and foremost . . . the Church as a whole.[52]

In Rahner's approach, the dogmatic statements of the church develop as the revealed truth is explicated within the growing faith consciousness of the entire church: "The subject matter of faith is not merely a passive datum [*Object*] standing indifferently in opposition to faith itself, but is simultaneously the principle by which it is in itself grasped as the subject matter of faith."[53]

Rahner proposed a way of describing the content of revelation that includes both its propositional and nonpropositional characteristics: The content of revelation is the "formal communication" of God to the transcendental subjectivity of the church.[54] To say that revelation is "formally communicated" is to say that the entire *revelatum* is communicated to the faith consciousness of the whole church in all the church's various forms of life as God continues to communicate in grace with human beings in the church. Part of revelation is known propositionally, but most of it is known prepropositionally and unthematically in the course of this ongoing formal communication. While a dogmatic development may appear to be the logical explication of what is formally *stated* in revelation (the neo-scholastic position), in fact dogmatic development is the result of the self-explication of the formally communicated *revelatum* within the faith consciousness of the church, and this explication takes place in various historical and cultural settings.

Although Rahner's project was based on the categories of a transcendental theology, it built on Newman's project in three ways. First, dogma itself is understood as a type of symbol that mediates and embodies that which it expresses. As for Newman, dogma is the articulation of an ongoing process of sifting, sorting, and discern-

[52] Rahner, "Considerations on the Development of Dogma," 32 (German, 47).

[53] Rahner, "Development of Dogma," 51 (German, 62).

[54] Rahner attributes the material basis of this distinction between "formally stated" and "formally communicated" revelation to E. Dhanis, "Révélation explicite et implicite," *Gregorianum* 34 (1953): 187–237. Also see Rahner, "Development of Dogma," 71n.

ing the message of revelation within specific historical and cultural situations. For Rahner, however, dogma is also understood philosophically as a symbol that unifies because it embodies that which it communicates. It is an event of "discourse" in the Heideggerian sense, and as symbol shares in the characteristics of language, but is not for that reason propositional matter alone. As we have seen, Newman did not intend to limit dogma to propositional matter either, and he included a range of data within the dogmatic field, as we have seen. However, Rahner's category of symbol offers a metaphysical criterion whereby these various dogmatic expressions can be understood under a common rubric, the prime analogate of which is the dogmatic proposition. We can thus extrapolate his analysis of the dogmatic proposition to the wider field of dogma which we are assuming here.

Second, the "mind of the church" plays a major role in arriving at formulations of dogma. For Rahner, this mind or faith consciousness is an abiding reality corresponding to the abiding offer of God's grace to human beings, spiritual subjects, who together constitute the church. Dogma will unify not only because it can be demonstrated that there is an organic linkage between later expressions and earlier ones, but also because the experience of faith itself, understood now as the transcendental relationship between the spiritual subjectivity of the church and the grace of God's self-communication to it, is a constant of human experience in history. The historicity of transcendental experience will mean that the faith consciousness of the church is realized within and through particular historical and cultural mediations. Moving beyond Newman, Rahner elaborated the historicity of faith consciousness as the knowing subjectivity of the entire church which hears, questions, and appropriates the self-communication of God in faith.

Third, the spiritual subjects of the church together, in their cultural variety and specificity, engage in the search for the truth communicated in revelation, a truth that receives a normative interpretation and articulation by the magisterium. For Newman, this search took place through the *conspiratio pastorum et fidelium*. For Rahner this search becomes the "collective finding of truth," where *ecclesia docens* and *ecclesia discens* together engage in the dialogue of faith, hearing, and questioning the self-communication of God in Jesus Christ as it is symbolically mediated in the life of the church. The grounds for agreement about the truth rest in part on the processes by which people of the church engage in this dialogue with the truth that is continually communicated to the church and symbolically mediated. The church, like the individual,

> reflects on the message—given by and received from Jesus Christ and transmitted in the belief of the primitive church—in relation to each particular, historically conditioned situation and based on her consciousness of faith and its original source. She reflects on this message and proclaims the one permanent faith anew in the form of this new theological reflection, with the decisive result that this faith retains and acquires anew as unavoidable a presence as possible for the one who hears the message.[55]

This interpretation of the message which takes place in the dialogue of faith, of hearing and questioning the word, occurs in every historical period and in every particular place where the church is found; it is an ongoing and never-finished activity of faith. The organic development of dogma proposed by Newman thus becomes transposed in Rahner to a question of the continuing reappropriation of the always-offered grace of revelation. This reappropriation occurs through with the unifying and mediating symbols of faith, for which the dogmatic statement stands as the prime analogue.

But now we must ask: How does this dialogue take place? How can dogma function as an instrument of unity within a church where this dialogue is occurring in many places, within different cultural settings, with specific interests, and often widely divergent viewpoints? This thrusts us into the universe implicitly opened up by Rahner, that of hermeneutics.

[55] Ibid., 53 (German, 67).

CHAPTER 4

Dogma as Classic of Tradition

[T]he horizon of the present cannot be formed without the past. There is no more an isolated horizon of the present in itself than there are historical horizons which have to be acquired. Rather, understanding is always the fusion of these horizons supposedly existing by themselves. . . . In a tradition this process of fusion is continually going on, for there old and new are always combining into something of living value.

—Hans-Georg Gadamer[1]

Rahner's project returns us to the main question with which we began: how dogma can serve as an instrument of catholic unity when, as an expression of the content of the experience of one faith, it is transmitted and appropriated by the multiple perspectives that constitute the communion of faith in a world church. We began by considering the function of dogma as the "idea" of revelation in Newman, which was a rhetorical construction. We then turned to dogma as symbol of the experience of God's self-communication in Rahner, a notion built on transcendental categories. Both of these focused on what was transmitted, the *revelatum*. Dogma faithfully transmitted the *revelatum* and thereby served as source of ecclesial consensus. Now we turn to the means of transmission and the process of appropriation of the life of faith, to

[1] Hans-Georg Gadamer, *Truth and Method*, 2d rev. ed., trans. Joel Weinsheimer and Donald G. Marshall (New York: Crossroad, 1989), 306; originally published as *Wahrheit und Methode: Grundzüge einer philosophischen Hermeneutik* (Tübingen: J. C. B. Mohr, 1975), 289–90.

tradition. This moves us beyond the rhetorical realm of Newman and the transcendental categories of Rahner into the world of hermeneutics, which is concerned with how we come to understand anything and derive meaning from it. The question now becomes: How can dogma itself be understood as a unifying factor within the tradition of faith, not only in what it faithfully transmits but in its manner of transmitting?

This question breaks out into three more specific questions. First, how can dogma, understood in a rich sense that includes but is not limited to propositional matter, reflect the pluralism of faith experiences and speak with authority to the "minds" or horizons of faith that constitute the church catholic? I will suggest that when dogma is understood as a classic, it can operate as a unifying focal point. In this regard, I will examine Hans-Georg Gadamer's presentation of the classic as a hermeneutical category in his magnum opus, *Truth and Method.* I am not claiming that all dogmas are classics, nor that dogma as a genre is classical, but rather that Gadamer's hermeneutics invites us to consider how dogma could function as a classic, in the way the local churches approach dogmatic expressions and search for a basis of catholic unity. The notion of the classic offers a vehicle for the ongoing interpretation of the dogmas of the faith tradition while safeguarding the essential core of the tradition transmitted in and represented by the classic itself.

How this unifying function is actually realized is our second question. For Gadamer, the classic transmits a tradition and draws various horizons into focus around it to the degree that it is engaged by interpreters through dialogue with it. In Gadamer's view of hermeneutical experience, a current horizon of understanding is addressed by the horizon of an authoritative tradition. The horizons of the present and of the past encounter each other in and through a specific subject matter offered by the horizon of the past, and consequently enter into intimate contact. The act of understanding is an effort by someone to grasp something that seems either alien to or vanished from one's immediate horizon of understanding. In the intimacy of contact between the two horizons, past meanings are mediated by present historical consciousness. The horizons of the familiar and the strange not only intermingle but give rise to a new horizon of meaning within present consciousness. When the subject matter for this fusion of horizons focuses on a classic of a tradition, this fusion of horizons results in the transmission and appropriation of the tradition that speaks through the classic. In the act of understanding, a person engages in one of the most basic of historical acts: entering into the transmission of a tradition and drawing it into one's own world. "Understanding is to be thought of less as a subjective act than as participating in an event of tradition, a process of transmission in which past and present are constantly mediated.[2]

But before pursuing this notion of dogma as classic and the role of dialogue in its function, we first need to inquire into the meaning of "hermeneutical experience," a notion upon which Gadamer's entire approach rests. Rahner's focus was primarily on the dogmatic statement, but he approached it from the standpoint of what he termed the "transcendental experience" of faith. Gadamer, however, speaks of "hermeneutical experience." What is meant by this term, and what is its relation to language and, more generally, to dogma as a theme of faith? Before embarking into the world of Gadamer's hermeneutics as a model for dogmatic unity, it would be well to look further into the relationship between experience and language that characterizes hermeneutical experience, and to see where Gadamer comes down on the issue.

HERMENEUTICAL EXPERIENCE AND LANGUAGE

In the previous chapter we noted that Lindbeck criticized Rahner's treatment of the relationship between religious experience and language. We return to the issue again, this time in relation to Gadamer. In *The Nature of Doctrine* Lindbeck sets forth three models for the ordering of religious experience and religious language. The first of these models, the cognitivist approach, "stresses the ways in which church doctrines function as informative propositions or truth claims about objective realities."[3] For example, the language of the Nicene Creed, which describes a consubstantial relation between Jesus Christ and the Father, is a faithful rendering of an objective reality known in faith, the singular relationship between Jesus and the God of Israel. Experience here is epistemo-

---

[2] Gadamer, *Truth and Method*, 290 (German, 274–75).
[3] Lindbeck, *Nature of Doctrine*, 16.

logically drawn, a matter of what can be known of revelation and rendered through intellectual judgment into language.

A second model, which Lindbeck calls the experiential-expressive approach, equates experience with "inner feelings, attitudes, or existential orientations," and the language of doctrine with "noninformative and nondiscursive symbols" of these vague inner feelings. Lindbeck seems to have in mind here facile or popular renderings of existential theologians such as P. Tillich or M. Buber, and, seemingly, transcendental theologians like Rahner. In any case, he tells us, "[e]xperiential expressivism has lost ground everywhere except in most theological schools and departments of religious studies where, if anything, the trend is the reverse."[4] The implication is that a rather complacent religiosity thrives in those locales, one which is not seriously concerned with the proper ordering of religious experience and religious discourse, and which takes for granted a certain aesthetic and emotional sense of what religious experience is. Language is a secondary phenomenon, accidentally related to the inner experience.

Lindbeck proposes a third model, the cultural-linguistic approach. Here, he tells us, "emphasis is placed on those respects in which religions resemble languages," language not only as grammar but "together with their correlative forms of life" (liturgies, rituals, practices, customs, traditions, beliefs, practices, etc.) such that religions resemble cultures. Thus, religions are subject to "thick description," and no one religious experience can exhaustively convey what a religion is about.[5] Indeed, the ordering of religion as a kind of culture comes from language; language does not issue from the experience of religion. Hence, "[t]he function of church doctrines that becomes most prominent in this perspective is their use, not as expressive symbols or truth claims, but as communally authoritative rules of discourse, attitude, and action."[6] In this model, language is an a priori condition of experience, not as subsequent articulation or expression of experience:

---

[4] Ibid., 25.

[5] See Clifford Geertz on "thick description" of cultures, in *The Interpretation of Cultures: Selected Essays* (New York: Basic Books, 1973).

[6] Lindbeck, *Nature of Doctrine*, 18.

... the means of communication and expression are a precondition, a kind of quasi-transcendental (i.e., culturally formed) *a priori* for the possibility of experience. We cannot identify, describe, or recognize experience qua experience without the use of signs and symbols. ... In short it is necessary to have the means for expressing an experience in order to have it, and the richer our expressive or linguistic system, the more subtle, varied, and differentiated can be our experience.[7]

As noted in the last chapter, Lindbeck claims that this position is at odds with that major part of the theological tradition represented by Karl Rahner and the transcendental Thomists.

Lash's Reply to Lindbeck's Critique

Nicholas Lash makes a significant contribution to this discussion of the relationship between experience and language in his *Easter in Ordinary*. Like Lindbeck, Lash is uneasy with the tendency, which he traces to William James, of speaking about religious experience "as if the 'essence' of personal religion was to be sought in abstraction from all considerations of structure, narrative, history and social relations."[8] Even basic words such as "God" are terms that regulate the activity whereby we critically interpret "the cultural, historical processes which produced us, and in which we find ourselves situated."[9] A word like "God," and the rest of doctrinal language, serves a "'set of protocols against idolatry,' against the manifold forms of the illusion that the nature of God lies within our grasp."[10] Generally agreeing with Lindbeck's cultural-linguistic approach, Lash argues that "the concept of the Christian doctrine of God be taken to refer to the declaration, by the Christian community, of identity-sustaining rules of discourse and behavior governing Christian uses of the word 'God.'"[11]

Unlike Lindbeck, however, Lash is not interested in merely reversing the inner–outer ordering of the relationship between

---

[7] Ibid., 36–37.
[8] Lash, *Easter in Ordinary*, 61.
[9] Ibid., 127.
[10] Ibid., 261.
[11] Ibid., 260.

experience and language. He insightfully notes Rahner's rejection of the idea that the doctrinal elements of Christian faith are merely the result of a subsequent reflection on the transcendental salvific relationship of humans to God.[12] If he could, Lash would abolish the category of "religious" experience altogether, in order to avoid the impression that such experience "may be phenomenologically distinguished from *other* kinds of conscious experience."[13] Instead, he would claim that what we call religious experience, like all experience, is essentially "hermeneutical." It is here especially that Lash is of interest to us, as his use of this term "hermeneutical" therefore requires some clarification.

First, he means that the relationship between religious experience and religious language is found in the dialectic of interpretation. Here, as we shall see, the voice of Gadamer comes through. The dialectic of interpretation begins with human participation in the totality of a religious tradition, not only in particular experiences labeled religious.

> God is to be known, not by "gazing" at representations of that movement (whether these be pictorial, narrative, or abstract in character) but by *participating* in it. And it is this participation which constitutes the reality of human life and history, a reality which achieves representational expression in Christian symbolism.[14]

We cannot begin to understand the life of faith unless we stand within it, namely, within the tradition that transmits it. It is an interpretive act that reworks the effect of experience itself by putting

> into fresh, accurate, and accessible language . . . stories and symbols that have—through use, misuse, and dislocation from the common conversation of the culture—become, in fact (for Christians and non-Christians alike) an obstacle to that hearing and proclamation of the Gospel of which they remain, nevertheless, the indispensable medium.[15]

Each generation has to rework the language of faith, and new aspects of meaning become evident in the process of doing so. The emphases and highlights of the life of faith that emerge as it is inter-

---

[12] Ibid., 129.
[13] Ibid.
[14] Ibid., 111.
[15] Ibid., 174.

preted are usually reflected in those dimensions of faith that receive popular expression. For example, the reconciling effect of the eucharist ("the Lamb of God who takes away the sins of the world") is a dimension of that sacrament's meaning that has been gained in recent years, while other dimensions, such as the eucharist as reenacted sacrifice, have generally waned.[16]

Second, "hermeneutical" implies a "mutually critical correlation" between participation and language in the interpretation of experiences. For, in this case, the accounts that we give, the interpretations that we offer, are an internally constitutive feature of that experience and make a difference to the experience itself. Christian experience is not the same experience as Jewish, Muslim, or secular experience, simply pushed through a distinctive Christian filter and thus differently described. In each of these cases, experience is modified by the interpretations that we offer, the memories to which we appeal in the stories that we tell.[17] Each is irreducibly distinctive. There is no "pure" experience apart from the interpretation of it, and, it could be added, there is no pure experience apart from the language in which this interpretation is made. While there can be no such experience of understanding apart from language, the relationship between that experience and language is not simply a matter of translation from one medium of meaning to another. It is rather one of mutual conditioning of experience and language. Lash's position here is similar to that taken by Edward Schillebeeckx, who traces a reciprocal relationship between experience ("the ability to assimilate perceptions") and the "already given framework of interpretation," which, in experience, "is exposed to criticism and corrected, changed or renewed by new experiences. . . . We experience in the act of interpreting, without being able to draw a neat distinction between the element of experience and the element of interpretation."[18] As we shall see, this mutual conditioning of expe-

---

[16] See Edward Kilmartin, "The Catholic Tradition of Eucharistic Theology: Towards the Third Millennium," *Theological Studies* 55 (1994): 405–57.

[17] Lash, *Easter in Ordinary*, 248–49.

[18] Edward Schillebeeckx, *Christ: The Experience of Jesus as Lord* (New York: Crossroad, 1989), 31–33. A similar insight, Lash tells us, can be found in Rahner, where revelation is the "answer" to the "question" that a human being is. Revelation is not some mysterious process that occurs solely at the transcendental level which then receives a subsequent objec-

rience and the language of interpretation comes about in what Gadamer means by dialogue. Propositional statements, dogmas per se, are one result. But the background for this relationship between dogma and what it expresses is based on the prior reality of an ongoing dialogue between the interpreter and what he or she experiences. Removed from a dialogic context, dogma becomes dead letter.

Understanding in and through Language

Lash is echoing here Gadamer's sentiments about hermeneutical experience. For Gadamer, the condition for the possibility of this transmission of tradition in and through the act of understanding is the fact that the world of the hermeneutical subject is a world of language. "Language is the fundamental mode of operation of our being-in-the-world and the all embracing form of the constitution of the world."[19] More than the secondary objectification or symbolizing of the meanings that arise in hermeneutical experience, language is the medium by which we exist as human subjects and is, therefore, the medium of hermeneutical experience. There is no historical existence, nor any hermeneutical experience apart from language. Not only is our hermeneutical experience realized in language, but this experience cannot be abstracted from language. Correlatively, our world is not only understood through the medium of language; it is itself language. Language is the common medium that makes possible a communication from one time-bound world to another and from one hermeneutical subject to another.

Language makes possible the "contemporaneity" of the past in the present, not merely the reconstruction of the past. "Contemporaneity" means that the text has meaning not merely as a monu-

---

tification in human speech, but is rather the name for that experience where the human subject receives an answer to the question that he or she is, and where this "answer" is interpreted within the languages of cultures and histories. These languages, in turn, are shaped by the answer itself.

[19] Hans-Georg Gadamer, "On the Universality of the Hermeneutical Problem," in *Philosophical Hermeneutics*, trans. and ed. David E. Linge (Berkeley: University of California Press, 1976), 4. Cf. *Truth and Method*, 395–405 (German, 373–82).

ment of the past but specifically in the current act of understanding it, and that this fact is the condition for its continuing effectiveness in history. Gadamer explains the religious force of this concept:

> For Kierkegaard, "contemporaneity" does not mean "existing at the same time." Rather, it names the task that confronts the believer: to bring together two moments that are not concurrent, namely one's own present and the redeeming act of Christ, and yet so totally to mediate them that the latter is experienced and taken seriously as present (and not as something in a distant past).[20]

In our encounter with specific languages "of an entirely different historical and cultural origin," we are introduced "to an experience of world which we had previously lacked and for which we lacked the words."[21] As we find the words, the thing that is spoken from the past, often in another language, appears for us within our current horizon of understanding. It comes to be in language. In our encounter with it, we do not just encounter a foreign utterance, translate it, interpret it, and then describe it. "Rather, within our language relationship to the world, that which is spoken of is itself first articulated through language's constitutive structuring of our being in the world."[22] Human existence is so bound up with language that the very understanding of any part of existence, including alien horizons of the past, is a linguistic event. Gadamer condenses this idea into the now well known dictum, "Being that can be understood is language."[23] But what does this mean? How is language itself to be understood as it functions? Here we turn to Gadamer's understanding of language as both "speculative" and "dialectical."

Gadamer characterizes the language that expresses hermeneutical experience as "speculative" because, as in great poetry, finite words can only mirror a reality far larger than themselves; like the image reflected by a mirror, where the image is always more than the reflection can show, words only begin to manifest the incalcu-

---

[20] Gadamer, *Truth and Method*, 127–28 (German, 121–22).

[21] Hans-Georg Gadamer, "Hegel and the Dialectic of the Ancient Philosophers," in *Hegel's Dialectic*, trans. P. Christopher Smith (New Haven: Yale University Press, 1976), 115–16.

[22] Ibid., 115.

[23] Gadamer, *Truth and Method*, 474 (German, 450).

lable vastness of the reality they attempt to express.[24] A surplus of meaning is therefore contained in each new expression of understanding, and each expression of understanding anticipates a wider range of meanings than can be captured in any one moment. No single expression of understanding can be considered definitive because no linguistic construction, with the possible exception of some great poetry, escapes the tension between the finite historical character of the interpreter's language and the virtual infinitude of truth toward which the language of interpretation aspires. This means that understanding through language will always involve a dialectic: hermeneutical experience is "dialectical" because the event of understanding itself involves a back-and-forth relationship between the horizon of the hermeneutical subject who questions and the horizon of the tradition that is questioned in and through a traditionary object of understanding, for example, the Bible or the Nicene Creed. Even when a new horizon is formed in the act of understanding, language can express only part of the meaning of this new horizon, and only part of the subjective experience of understanding it. A wealth of unspoken meanings lodged in the new horizon of the textual tradition remains unexpressed. Some, but not all, of these unspoken meanings will be uncovered in further questioning of the traditionary object, but others will fade into the background or remain concealed entirely.

Implications of Gadamer's Project for Dogma

Because the language of hermeneutical experience is both speculative and dialectical, Gadamer devalues the declarative, objectifying statement that would try to clearly describe this experience or would in effect translate into language the truth unveiled in hermeneutical experience:

> What is true of every word in which thought is expressed, is true also of the interpreting word, namely that it is not, as such, objective. As the realization of the act of understanding it is the actuality of historically effected consciousness, and as such it is truly speculative:

---

[24] Ibid., 465–74 (German, 441–49).

having no tangible being of its own and yet reflecting the image that is presented to it.[25]

The objectifying statement is therefore a secondary phenomenon in relation to hermeneutical experience itself. Hermeneutical experience does not simply begin with one objectifying statement and end up with another. The starting point for hermeneutical experience is broader, as is its end: it is simply being in the world wherein one encounters various subject matters. The result of the act of understanding includes objectifying statements, but these are placed within a horizon of understanding that extends beyond them and is essentially open-ended. On the matter of the relationship between experience and language, this would seem to put Gadamer in Lindbeck's experiential-expressivist camp, along with Rahner.[26] Gadamer, however, works not from transcendental categories but from hermeneutical ones rooted in the nature of language itself.

In taking this approach to the hermeneutical enterprise, Gadamer stands somewhat in contrast to those approaches to understanding that would insist on the priority of the object of understanding—for example, a proposition—and would grant a certain objective status to the message that the proposition conveys to the interpreter. One of Gadamer's earliest interlocutors, Emilio Betti, criticized Gadamer's approach for giving too much leeway to the interpreter and not enough to the objective status of the text.[27]

---

[25] Ibid., 473–74 (German, 449).

[26] For an important criticism of Gadamer on this point, see Wolfhart Pannenberg, "Hermeneutic and Universal History," in *Basic Questions in Theology*, trans. George Kehm (London: SCM, 1970), 96–136, who argues that the transmission of the Christian faith tradition depends on both the larger context within which propositions are made and the propositions themselves. He suggests that Gadamer's approach leans too heavily on the presumption of a common context within which divergent horizons of understanding might converge around a common subject matter. R. Nicholas Davey points out that in the absence of some propositional mapping, there can be no understanding if the subject matter itself is at issue. See "A Response to P. Christopher Smith," in *Continental Philosophy IV: Gadamer and Hermeneutics*, ed. Hugh J. Silverman (New York: Routledge, 1991), 42–59.

[27] See Richard Palmer, *Hermeneutics: Interpretation Theory in Schleiermacher, Dilthey, Heidegger, and Gadamer* (Evanston, Ill.: Northwestern, 1969), 54–60.

What we must strive for, he maintained, is an objectively valid interpretation. This alternative approach to hermeneutics is also reflected in those who would hold that the Constitution of the United States harbors an objective meaning, in this case a meaning intended by the Framers, which it is the duty of judges to discern and apply apart from the changing contours of contemporary circumstances. It is also reflected in the view that dogma, understood as the authoritative teaching of the church expressed in formal declarations, enjoys an objective status that admits of only limited interpretation and local application. Gadamer does not at all intend to deny the objective validity of propositions, but he wants to place them within a wider context, a whole world of experience that they rest within and partly express. The Nicene Creed, for example, does have an objective status. But if we want to understand the meaning of faith, we do not ordinarily begin with an interpretation of the creed; rather we begin with the experience of faith of which the creed is an inalienable expression.

The relationship between understanding and language which Gadamer establishes carries with it two important implications. First, hermeneutical experience is made universal. The universality of hermeneutical experience refers not to the mastery of a specific technical method for understanding but rather to the unlimited possibility of "an encounter with something that asserts itself as truth."[28] "Truth" here does not mean an empirically verifiable assertion, but rather (in the Heideggerian sense) the appearance of something in our horizon of understanding simply as it is for us. The truth of the Gospels, for example, is not limited only to what historical science can verify as having occurred in the life of Jesus. The truth of the Gospels is the unveiling in Jesus Christ (who is the truth [*aletheia*, John 14:6] of God) as He is for us. And this truth is profoundly historical because it occurs within and constitutes history. For example, the historical truth of the Resurrection extends far beyond any possible reconstruction of the "mechanics" of Jesus' passage from biological to glorified life. Yet the Resurrection is an event that occurred in space and time, which, moreover, reveals the power of God in a way that extends even beyond the time of the apostles themselves. Indeed, it was and remains the very basis of

---

[28] Gadamer, *Truth and Method*, 489 (German, 463).

faith. This is a historical truth, the meaning of which is not adequately determined on the basis of efforts at empirical verification.

That which asserts itself as truth does not necessarily come to us as a text or even in grammatical form, but it does "address" us, and our understanding of it is linguistic. Second, the meaning of truth in understanding is not confined to the most faithful reconstruction of an originally intended meaning. It refers instead to the integration of the horizon of the current interpreter with the horizon of the tradition which addresses him, and the unveiling of a new horizon of meaning. This event of understanding is an event of language, even though the actual objectifying statement of it is secondary in temporal sequence. All of this supports the concern of this book to understand dogma as a mode of faith confession, not only as a proposition of church teaching.

With this much background on hermeneutical experience itself, we can now approach Gadamer's treatment of the classic as it is understood within hermeneutical experience.

ENCOUNTERING THE CLASSIC

In order to imagine how dogma might function as a "classic," we need to situate the notion of the classic within Gadamer's thought. This is not the occasion to rehearse the whole of Gadamer's philosophical hermeneutics, which he summarizes at the beginning of *Truth and Method*:

> [T]he following investigation starts with a critique of aesthetic consciousness in order to defend the experience of truth that comes to us through the work of art against the aesthetic theory which lets itself be restricted to a scientific concept of truth. But the book does not rest content with justifying the truth of art; instead, it tries to develop from this starting point a conception of knowledge and of truth that corresponds to the whole of our hermeneutic experience. Just as in the experience of art we are concerned with truths that go essentially beyond the range of methodical knowledge, so the same thing is true of the human sciences: in them our historical tradition in all its forms is certainly made the *object* of investigation, but at the same time, *truth comes to speech in it.* Fundamentally, the experience of historical tradition reaches far beyond those aspects of it that can be objectively investigated. It is true or untrue not only in the sense

concerning which historical criticism decides, but always mediates truth in which one must *try to share*.[29]

In view of this kind of project, we must ask how certain aspects of Gadamer's philosophical project might inform our own, especially in his use of the "classic." Here I will focus on three aspects of his project: (1) the "moment of application," (2) the historicity of understanding, and (3) the authority of tradition. These three principles frame Gadamer's understanding of the classic as it operates within a tradition. I will later propose that what is valid of a classic here is also valid of dogma as a theme of faith.

Three Hermeneutical Principles

1. THE MOMENT OF APPLICATION

The "moment of application" refers to the fact that any classic, such as a dogma, is a monument of tradition that speaks from the past directly into the situation of the interpreter. It therefore speaks to and is received and understood within a particular contemporary context, the local setting of the interpreter in the present moment. The act of understanding thus presumes a context of current time, or of history, where the horizon of the past encounters the horizon of the present. The present moment of understanding is conditioned by the past, but the past is also conditioned by the present of understanding. For example, Beethoven's *Fidelio* could be understood as an operatic classic expressing certain ideals of the Enlightenment period. It conveys to the current horizon a view of the supremacy of human freedom from that particular historical epoch. On the other hand, our own historical experience in the two hundred years since *Fidelio* was composed, particularly our witnessing of the continuing struggles for freedom around the world, shed a certain light on *Fidelio* which Beethoven's audiences could not have anticipated.

Gadamer argues that this sense of historicity has been lost in a breathless search for "scientific" modes of understanding—understanding that prescinds from the current context in the search for some timeless, objective meaning. He specifies the task of philo-

---

[29] Gadamer, "Introduction," in *Truth and Method*, xxiii (German, xxix).

sophical hermeneutics as one of overcoming "the epistemological
truncation by which the traditional 'science of hermeneutics' has
been absorbed into the idea of modern science."[30] In a specific reference to the influence of the hermeneutical methods inspired by
Friedrich Schleiermacher, he adds that philosophical hermeneutics
aims "to transcend the prejudices that underlie . . . the hermeneutical consciousness that has been restricted to a technique for avoid-
ing misunderstandings."[31] He is referring here to methods of
interpretation developed especially in the Enlightenment and
Romantic periods, in which various quasi-scientific methodological
techniques were proposed in order to enter into the inner works of
a text. In theology, this ultimately took the form of historical-criti-
cal exegesis and research into the origins, history, literary form, and
rhetorical structure of the biblical texts. The distinction between
sacred text and classic text was collapsed under the hegemony of
the various techniques of "scientific" interpretation aimed at pro-
curing objective meanings inhering in the text.[32] As noted earlier, a
correlative trend in the understanding of dogma was evident in the
centuries following the Council of Trent: the delimitation of the
notion of dogma into discrete propositions subject to the precise
analyses of rational theology and uncritically identified with the
full content of revelation itself, leaving little room for interpretation
beyond logical analysis. Even after Newman, the hermeneutics of
dogma shared in this quasi-scientific bent of rationalism, represented especially by the neo-Thomist projects.

Two types of hermeneutical consciousness—aesthetic and historical consciousness—typify the absorption of hermeneutics into the
ideal of modern science. Quasi-scientific methods of interpreting
both art and history resulted in the disconnection of specific
aspects of a given tradition not only from their historical origins
but from history itself. The art of understanding such subject mat-

[30] Ibid., 3 (German, 1).
[31] Gadamer, "On the Universality of the Hermeneutical Problem," 7–8;
see also *Truth and Method*, "Introduction," xxi (German, xxvii).
[32] On the distinction between sacred and profane, see Gadamer, *Truth
and Method*, 150 (German, 142–45) and, especially in regard to scripture,
173–84 (German, 162–72). See also Sandra M. Schneiders, *The Revelatory
Text: Interpreting the New Testament as Sacred Scripture* (San Francisco:
HarperSanFrancisco, 1991).

ter became dependent on the skill at hand in methodically analyzing and describing the subject matter and in reassembling the historical, psychological, and material conditions of its genesis. The modern museum was founded on the principle that art constitutes a reality that can be understood on its own terms, that it bears an intrinsic meaning, reflects societal codes, or is related to wider cultures in ways that can be understood with the proper methodological tools. Thus, art history increasingly becomes in part the archaeology of the object, removed from its original life setting, until the object itself is disassembled or deconstructed. This is true, too, of some works, even classics, that no longer reverberate as they once did because they are received into a culture that no longer understands them as part of the culture, but rather as artifacts of the past. One result of this severance of art from context is an "epistemological truncation" between the knowing effort of the interpreter and the subject matter itself. The horizons of the interpreter and of the subject matter never truly make contact; they rarely produce a genuinely new horizon of meaning.

The alienation of the subject matter from its own history results in an alienation of the interpreter from the subject matter. For example, as some parts of popular music culture demonstrate, symbols, including religious ones, have ceased to function in their original contexts. They have often degenerated into ciphers of piety or into mystagogic decoration for the uncomprehending or icons of a false nostalgia. Neither type of alienation, of the subject matter from its own history or of the interpreter from the subject matter, can be overcome if the effort toward understanding prescinds from either the tradition out of which the subject matter springs, or the contemporary context within which it is encountered. In the absence of tradition and contemporary context, we are left with a concept of knowledge and of truth which stands in isolation from the historicity of either the tradition of the subject matter or of the knower.

Closely related to this problem is the conventional separation of the "moment of application" (*Anwendung*) from the act of understanding itself. This can be traced to the influence of Romantic hermeneutics, which in its zeal to prevent misunderstandings by "scientifically" entering into the mind of the author, effectively ignored the fact that understanding is also the partial result of the "application" or situating of a subject matter within particular circumstances. Understanding takes place within a concrete contemporary context, not in abstraction from it. Gadamer holds that as the moment of application became isolated from the act of understanding and from the theory of hermeneutics, certain types of literature were robbed of their traditional edifying power as they became mere objects of literary or historical research. This was particularly true of scripture, where theological and historical understanding of scripture as a text could take place outside of the context of preaching, where scripture had normally been applied, understood, and interpreted.

Gadamer reasserts "application" as an integral part of hermeneutical endeavor.[33] Gadamer is not arguing that acquired meanings be tested by experience, for example, in the way learning theories might be tested by application to concrete situations. He is urging, rather, that the act of understanding be seen as taking place within the existential situation of the interpreter. For example, one's current interest in the meaning of the Chalcedonian Definition need not be philological alone, nor merely historical or archaeological reconstruction, important as these endeavors can be. It may very possibly arise out of the particular questions that occur to the Christian consciousness in a time when the Greek philosophical tradition is no longer a familiar one to most people, when questions arise about the meaning of traditional terminology, or where the presuppositions of Christian tradition about Jesus encounter the tenets of non-Christian cultures and religions.

Legal hermeneutics demonstrates the integral role played by the moment of application in the act of understanding. Understanding a legal utterance of the past cannot merely amount to repeating past formulas: it must involve a participation by the subject in the constitution of the present meaning of the past in a particular case:

> Legal hermeneutics serve to remind us what the real procedure of the human sciences is. Here we have the model for the relationship between past and present that we are seeking. The judge who adapts the transmitted law to the needs of the present is undoubtedly seeking to perform a practical task, but his interpretation of the law is by no means merely for that reason an arbitrary new interpretation. . . .

[33] Gadamer, *Truth and Method*, 308–11 (German, 290–95).

The work of interpretation is to concretize the law in each specific case—i.e., it is the work of application.[34]

In the moment of application, a normative meaning of a past legal utterance becomes focused within a current horizon of understanding. It thus becomes operative within a current existential situation. The person who interprets and understands such a legal utterance from the past places himself within the legal tradition that speaks to one through it; the legal utterance becomes the medium of the transmission of the legal tradition. Moreover, the current interpreter (e.g., the judge) assists in the creative application of the "old" meanings of a law to present circumstances. As a result, apparently new meanings or shades of meaning can arise.

2. THE HISTORICITY OF UNDERSTANDING

By the "historicity of understanding" Gadamer refers to the continuing influence on the act of understanding itself of a tradition of interpretation, a tradition to which each new act of understanding contributes. In underscoring the importance of historicity, Gadamer is stressing the idea that the events of history constitute a tradition within which observers already stand even as they try to understand these events.

> If we are trying to understand an historical phenomenon from the historical distance that is characteristic of our hermeneutical situation, we are always already affected by history. It determines in advance both what seems to us worth inquiring about and what will appear to us as an object of investigation, and we more or less forget what is really there—in fact, we miss the whole truth of the phenomenon—when we take its immediate appearance as the whole truth.[35]

The effects of the history of a tradition work directly on one's current effort to understand anything of that tradition. Moreover, the act of understanding becomes a part of the history of the subject matter itself. Thus, for example, classical formulations of faith such as the Chalcedonian Definition are subject to ever renewed theological analyses in the attempt to render them comprehensible within contemporary forms of thought and culture. No current

---

[34] Ibid., 327–30 (German, 311–13).
[35] Ibid., 230 (German, 284).

effort to understand Chalcedon can ignore fifteen centuries of interpretation that have already been accomplished and come bearing down on the present moment, nor the practice of faith in Jesus Christ that gives witness to the weight of this tradition. Contemporary efforts at understanding Chalcedon, however, can contribute to the overall interpretational tradition of the Definition, as, for example, did Rahner's treatment of it in his famous essay in 1951, in which he tried to counter Monophysite renderings of it.[36] The current debates over Spirit Christology could well portend a further benchmark in the way the history of the Definition functions in every new act of understanding it.[37]

A further point in describing an "effective history of interpretation" is to suggest that the difference between past and present renderings of a monument of the tradition are not unbridgeable. The past continues to work within the present because the present brings to the act of understanding a history of interpretation that functions in such a way as to keep the past alive. The genius of Bach's "Goldberg Variations," for example, has been kept alive in part because of the effect of the history of interpretations given them, from Bach himself, all the way through Glenn Gould and his interpretive successors. Thus, the effective history of interpretation actually bridges the hermeneutical distance that quasi-scientific theories would simply eliminate as an obstacle to understanding. The difference between past and present is thus turned into a positive element in the act of understanding.

Consciousness of this history of the effects of tradition on the current act of understanding includes consciousness of the context created by the tradition within which we stand. In most every case, however, it is a task of particular difficulty to acquire a clear awareness of where we stand; precisely because we stand within a tradition and not outside of it, we are unable to have a purely objective knowledge of it. Because one stands within the context of a tradition, understanding it will always be an unfinished labor, not

---

[36] Karl Rahner, "Current Problems in Christology," in *Theological Investigations*, vol. 1, trans. Cornelius Ernst (London: Darton, Longman & Todd, 1961), 149–200.

[37] See Roger Haight, "The Case for Spirit Christology," *Theological Studies* 53 (1992): 257–87, and a response by John H. Wright, "Roger Haight's Spirit Christology," *Theological Studies* 53 (1992): 729–35.

because of a deficiency in reflection itself but owing to the fact that we are contingent beings and the nature of understanding is itself inescapably finite.[38] The interpreter does not merely stand before the tradition as if the tradition itself were a collection of objects or a deposit of data. One stands within the tradition and, in a sense, belongs to it because one is claimed by it. When a believing Christian inquires into the meaning of a biblical text, for example, that person stands within the biblical tradition, never fully outside of it. "Hermeneutics must proceed from the principle that a person seeking to understand something has a bond to the subject matter that comes into language through the traditionary text and has, or acquires, a connection with the tradition from which the text speaks."[39] One's consciousness of the fact that the act of understanding takes place within the history of the tradition itself is the first step toward suspending the relation of distance or alienation one might feel toward the tradition. When this distance or alienation is suspended, the interpreter may be addressed by the tradition, or by parts of it.

3. THE AUTHORITY OF TRADITION

In connection with this concept of the historicity of understanding, Gadamer focuses on two concepts that he claims have been discredited since the Enlightenment: tradition and authority. Gadamer's use of the word "tradition" includes two elements that cannot be separated from each other: (1) the history of understanding shared by several subjects, and (2) the continuing self-manifestation of this history of understanding in the cultural components (artistic, linguistic, literary, religious, legal, etc.), which constitute the context for understanding anything. As David Linge explains Gadamer's use of the term, "[l]ike Heidegger's notion of being, tradition is not a thing existing somehow behind its disclosures. . . .[T]radition is precisely its happening, its continuing self-manifestations, much as Heidegger defines being as eventful, i.e., as disclosive rather than substantive."[40]

We always stand within a tradition when we understand any-

---

[38] Gadamer, *Truth and Method*, 301 (German, 285).

[39] Ibid., 295 (German, 279).

[40] David Linge, "Editor's Introduction," in *Philosophical Hermeneutics* (Berkeley: University of California Press, 1976), liv.

thing, even if we feel alienated from that tradition or are attempting to understand only a specific part of it. While we may attempt to understand totally exotic and foreign traditions, even this attempt takes place from the standpoint of one's position within one's own tradition and in a spirit of openness to the different or unknown. Traditions "happen" or, better, function as transmitting agents, precisely in the act of understanding what it is that they are transmitting. This understanding takes place

> in the interplay of the movement of the tradition and the movement of the interpreter. The anticipation of meaning that governs our understanding of a text is not an act of subjectivity, but proceeds from the commonality that binds us to the tradition. But this commonality is constantly being formed in our relation to tradition. Tradition is not simply a permanent precondition; rather, we produce it ourselves, inasmuch as we understand, participate in the evolution of tradition, and hence further determine it ourselves.[41]

Thus, tradition is a living thing, an ongoing reality with its own effective history. Gadamer believes that this is what the Enlightenment view of tradition lost sight of in its rejection of the authority of traditions.[42]

The Idea of the Classic

These three marks of Gadamer's thought—the moment of application, the historicity of understanding, and the authority of tradition—frame his understanding of the classic, to which we can now turn. For Gadamer, the concept of the classic has a "normative" and a "historical" connotation.[43] Normatively, the study of classical

---

[41] Gadamer, *Truth and Method*, 293 (German, 277).

[42] Ibid., 276–78 (German, 260–63).

[43] Ibid., 285–90 (German, 269–75). For a discussion of these terms, see Joel C. Weinsheimer, *Gadamer's Hermeneutics: A Reading of Truth and Method* (New Haven: Yale University Press, 1985), 174–75. See also treatments of the classic by David Tracy, *The Analogical Imagination: Christian Theology and the Culture of Pluralism* (New York: Crossroad, 1981), 99–299. For a discussion of the differences between Gadamer and Tracy on the classic, see Werner G. Jeanrond, *Text and Interpretation as Categories of Theological Thinking*, trans. Thomas J. Wilson (New York: Crossroad, 1988), 133–42.

antiquity, for example, proceeds through a reading and interpretation of certain works that constitute the classical canon. A part of the canon, in turn—for example, Sophocles—is understood as the plays of Sophocles have been understood through contextual studies in history, archaeology, philology, and other disciplines on the assumption that there is a classical period of history that continues to speak with interest, if not authority. Gadamer's point is that whereas many people associate the "classic" with an ideal past set in opposition to current modes of understanding the world, it is necessary to see the classic as more than a normative body of great works representing a historical epoch. The "historical" connotation of the classical should not imply a "suprahistorical" category for understanding old things or great things, as if the timelessness of the classics meant that they could not be interpreted with new insights today.

The classical as an interpretive category has meaning not only in and through its own monuments (e.g., the normative canon) but also through the current historical effort to keep it alive. The "classic" therefore refers to a concept that "resists historical criticism because its historical dominion, the binding power of the validity that is preserved and handed down, precedes all historical reflection and continues in it."[44] The classic is not only a voice from the past; it speaks within the present. It not only provides information about a time now defunct; it can illuminate current historical experience. It is not merely the object of grammatical and philological analysis; it is the real presence of the past communicating itself to us in various languages that can be understood. "What we call 'classical' does not first require the overcoming of historical distance, for in its own constant mediation it overcomes this distance by itself. The classical, then, is certainly 'timeless,' but this timelessness is a mode of historical being."[45] Gadamer's view here coincides with that of David Tracy, who writes:

> The classical text is not in some timeless moment which needs mere repetition. Rather its kind of timelessness as permanent timeliness is the only one proper to any expression of the finite, temporal, historical beings we are. The classic text's real disclosure is its claim to attention on the ground that an event of understanding proper to

[44] Gadamer, *Truth and Method*, 287 (German, 271).
[45] Ibid., 290 (German, 274).

finite human beings has here found expression. The classic text's fate is that only its constant reinterpretation by later finite, historical, temporal beings who will risk asking its questions and listening, critically and tactfully, to its responses can actualize the event of understanding beyond its present fixation in a text. Every classic lives as a classic only if it finds readers willing to be provoked by its claim and attention.[46]

The act of understanding a representative classical work, then, is not merely an effort of subjective consciousness, the solitary work of a scholar analyzing the objective language of a text; it is a placing of oneself in the tradition of the classic itself. In this act, which focuses on a particular work or monument of a tradition, the horizons of the present and of the past converge and give rise to new meaning and to the revitalization of the tradition represented by the classical text.

Transposing Dogma into the Classic

Transposing dogma into Gadamer's understanding of the classic enables us to imagine dogma functioning as a monument of the tradition of faith. Dogma as classic is an expression of the tradition of faith and is partly constitutive of it. It therefore shares in the historicity of the tradition. The faith tradition in which we stand speaks with an authority that claims our attention; indeed it does this partly through the various dogmatic expressions that carry this tradition. Dogma as classic thus shares in the history of the effects of the tradition upon us. The interpreter of this tradition confronts the tradition partly through these "classics." Dogma as classic therefore functions with a certain authority which invites our acceptance of its claim. People of faith bring to this confrontation a commitment to the intrinsic validity and truth of the message transmitted in the tradition and to the requirement that this message be understood anew in current situations. This commitment is tantamount to the conviction that the word once revealed continues to speak even in the classical monuments of the faith tradition, and that the church in its various historical particularities continues to hear this

___

[46] Tracy, *Analogical Imagination*, 102.

word anew, to appropriate and to understand it, thus building on the tradition.

Consideration of dogma's function as "classic" allows for both a normative and a flexible role of dogma in the life of faith. The classic carries a normative history of interpretation which any party, in this case, the church of a particular time and place, cannot ignore. On the other hand, the classic, like a Shakespeare play, is subject to ongoing interpretation and "performance" in the specificity of a particular time and place. The dialectic between the normative reading given the classic by the tradition, and the particular reading given through its "application" in a particular time and place is what gives life to the tradition. A tradition based only on normative readings would quickly become ossified; a tradition based only on local application would gradually disintegrate. A tradition read (and interpreted) simultaneously from a multiplicity of perspectives is a tradition that is being taken seriously as a living reality with a claim upon its adherents. It is also a tradition the "content" of which—that is, that which is handed down—remains substantially itself even as it is interpreted anew in each new ecclesial situation. What is true of the great monuments of faith (e.g., the creeds, the Chalcedonian Definition, etc.) may be true, analogously, of those dogmatic expressions which are not, strictly speaking, classics, but which nevertheless, within the hierarchy of truths, address the church with the authority of tradition: some liturgical formulae, canonized disciplines, or polities such as those governing ministers of baptism or candidates for ordination, the shape and mode of the exercise of primacy and episcopacy, and certain moral teachings.

But what is the context within which this understanding of dogma as classic takes place? How can many horizons of understanding, as we witness in the pluralism of the contemporary Catholic Church, find common ground in the dogmatic classic? The answer Gadamer offers is understanding through a "dialogue" between the classic and its interpreters, which leads to a new level of understanding, a fusion of horizons.

UNDERSTANDING THROUGH DIALOGUE

In *Gaudium et spes*, the Second Vatican Council recommended to the church the value of "dialogue" as a way the church might conduct itself in relation to culture, and also how the church itself might find unity:

> In virtue of its mission to spread the light of the gospel's message over the entire globe, and to bring all people of whatever nation, race or culture together into the one Spirit, the church comes to be a sign of that kinship which makes genuine dialogue possible and vigorous. This requires us first of all to promote mutual esteem, respect and harmony, with the recognition of all legitimate diversity, in the church itself, in order to establish ever more fruitful exchanges among all who make up the one people of God, both pastors and the rest of the faithful. For what unites the faithful is stronger than what divides them: there should be unity in essentials, freedom in doubtful matters, and charity in everything.[47]

The value of dialogue as the means of understanding dogma within a pluralistic situation is not to be underestimated. Some light can be shed on this notoriously slippery notion of "dialogue" if we examine it within the terms of Gadamer's philosophical hermeneutics. For Gadamer understanding is an intrinsically dialogical process. Dialogue with the tradition within which one stands is an indispensable element in the effort to understand anything belonging to that tradition.[48] In Gadamer's approach, understanding takes place through a dialogue between the interpreter and the subject matter through which the tradition speaks. The paradigm for understanding the monuments of tradition is understanding a classical text through reading it.[49] Gadamer explains:

> What characterizes a dialogue, in contrast with the rigid form of statements that demand to be set down in writing, is precisely this: that in dialogue spoken language—in the process of question and answer, giving and taking, talking at cross purposes and in seeing each other's point—performs that communication of meaning that, with respect to the written tradition, is the task of hermeneutics. Hence it is more than a metaphor—it is a memory of what originally was the case, to describe the task of hermeneutics as entering into dialogue with the text.[50]

---

[47] *Gaudium et spes,* 92, in *Decrees of the Ecumenical Councils,* 2:1134.

[48] For more on dialogue with the tradition, see Weinsheimer, *Gadamer's Hermeneutics,* 205.

[49] Gadamer, *Truth and Method,* 159–64 (German, 152–61).

[50] Ibid., 368 (German, 350).

What is true of understanding a classical text is true of understanding any part of tradition (art works, laws, dogmatic statements, etc.). The classical text is the utterance of a tradition. In order to understand the text and the tradition of which it is an utterance, one must receive what the text says within one's own historically conditioned consciousness. This means that one must listen to what the text is saying. In effect, one must engage in a dialogue with the text and the textual tradition. One allows the text to raise questions of meaning, and, in actively engaging the text, one in a sense responds to the questions the text raises. One anticipates where the text might lead. This hermeneutical relationship with the text, which rests in part upon allowing the text to claim us with the authority vested in it as a classic of tradition, results in the further determination of current meaning of the tradition that speaks through it.

Prejudices and Understanding

In the dialogic interplay between the interpreter and a classic of tradition, one finds oneself in possession of a pre-understanding (*Vorverständnis*) of the meaning of the subject matter of the tradition as presented in a text. Gadamer finds the basis for this idea of pre-understanding in the early Heidegger:

> Heidegger entered into the problem of historical hermeneutics and critique only in order to explicate the fore-structure of understanding for the purposes of ontology. . . . [E]very revision of the fore-projection is capable of projecting before itself a new projection of meaning; rival projects can emerge side by side until it becomes clearer what unity of meaning is; interpretation begins with the fore-conceptions that are replaced by more suitable ones. This constant process of new projection constitutes the movement of meaning in understanding and interpretation.[51]

This "pre-understanding" does not simply "begin" at a fixed point in one's dialogue with the text. It results in part from the framework of prejudices that the reader brings to a text, but also from the gradual composition of a definite "voice" from the past which becomes clearer as the reading and questioning advance. As in an

[51] Ibid., 165–67 (German, 150–52).

ordinary conversation, a range of possible meanings emerges "in advance," and finally one of these prevails as the strongest meaning. And this final meaning has already been anticipated, though not actually known or stated. It is pre-understanding that draws one further into interplay with the text so that one can receive and articulate its meaning.

Because understanding proceeds on the basis of pre-understandings, all understanding is characterized by pre-judgments or prejudices (*Vorurteile*) of meaning which qualify the meaning that finally emerges. Gadamer would turn the prejudices of the current historical standpoint from obstacles to understanding into positive factors in understanding.[52] The interpreter becomes conscious of the fact that the meaning of which one has a pre-understanding does not exist as a pure idea; nor can it be received or understood apart from the various conditions of understanding which shape the way we perceive reality in general. In short, our prejudices—the historical constellation of preconceptions, commitments, patterns of thinking, life experiences, and other concrete factors that shape our everyday experience—are a part of the historical conditionality of hermeneutical experience. Prejudices can become the object of reflexive awareness, but can rarely, if ever, be transcended to the point of playing no role in understanding. Prejudices are part of the makeup of the human subject (and communities of subjects). In the act of understanding, these prejudices are operative: they are brought to light, tested, and either ratified as conducive toward the pursuit of truth or rejected as obstacles to understanding. But no understanding is possible in abstraction from prejudices; there is no presuppositionless understanding. Even a dogmatic tradition, no matter how authoritatively presented, will be received outside the framework of prejudice.

Beyond this more or less neutral sense of prejudice as a set of presuppositions, Gadamer distinguishes between pejorative and positive connotations of the term. While prejudice can bear a pejorative meaning, as in the case of the inflexible application of a strict and possibly ossified prejudicial framework of meanings upon the act of interpretation such that the interpreter cannot in fact creatively understand a given tradition but only repeat or

---

[52] Ibid., 279–80 (German, 261–65).

rephrase past formulations ("dogmatic" in the everyday sense), it also has a positive sense.[53] Its positive sense denotes an a priori posture of commitment to the tradition and of openness to what it might say that is brought to the occasion of understanding by the interpreter of the subject matter of a tradition. The prejudice that scripture is the word of God that continues to speak to the church and hence requires new interpretations is quite different either from the prejudice of fundamentalism that scripture can yield no new interpretations, or even from the quasi-scientific prejudice that scripture be approached as if it were merely ancient literature whose meaning could be completely determined by methods of literary criticism or by historical analysis. Prejudice in Gadamer's more positive sense of commitment and openness can be operative in every act of understanding. Consequently, a commitment to the faith tradition that is transmitted in and through its classics is not necessarily to be taken in a pejorative sense. Such a commitment could ground an openness in favor of the possibility of continuing understanding of its great monuments.

From Common Ground to Truth

Gadamer maintains that the dialogue of the interpreter with the text closely resembles the dialectical structure of a Platonic dialogue.[54] The Platonic dialogue is a rational procedure aimed at the pursuit of truth. It assumes that two partners who do not initially share each other's views agree to meet on common ground. This common ground is that uncharted or strange space which lies between the respective horizons of the partners. One partner in the dialogue (the Socratic teacher) addresses the other partner and challenges the latter's opinions with subtle questions. But neither partner addresses the other as a mere object of interest. The rela-

---

[53] See Tracy, *Analogical Imagination*, 99–100.

[54] Ibid., 362–69 (German, 344–51). For further discussion of dialogue with the text, see David Couzens Hoy, *The Critical Circle: Literature, History and Philosophical Hermeneutics* (Berkeley: University of California Press, 1982), 65–68.

tion is one of subject to subject, of I to Thou.[55] The teacher in a sense becomes a student within the context of the dialogic exchange.

The classic of a tradition addresses the reader in much the same way. The person addressed by the classic text listens with a posture of both openness and prejudice toward what is said; she receives and sorts out what she hears. Yet in order to "hear" what is said in a conversation with the text, the hearer must allow for a momentary loss of self. In this momentary loss of self the reader renders herself open to the word, which in turn makes a kind of claim on her. The text is thus allowed to appear within one's own horizon of understanding. In the Platonic dialogue this happens as the Socratic partner poses a question to the other partner. This questioning keeps the dialogue open, but also sets certain limits to the direction of the dialogue. The Socratic partner is invested with a certain authority in the dialogue itself.

If the questioning is artfully posed, it will elicit a response, even if the response is only a nod of tacit agreement. Regardless of the form of response, the dialectical pattern of the dialogue is established as long as a mutual commitment to openness and the pursuit of meaning is maintained by both partners. The subject matter of the dialogue itself develops within the dialectical exchange. The aim of the dialogue is not that one of the partners win an argument; this is the aim of debate. It is rather the pursuit of truth starting from the common ground of the dialogue.

> What emerges in its truth . . . is neither mine nor yours and hence so far transcends the interlocutors' subjective opinions that even the person leading the conversation knows that he does not know. As the art of conducting a conversation, dialectic is also the art of seeing things in the unity of an aspect . . . i.e. it is the art of forming concepts through working out the common meaning. . . .[56]

The dialectical structure of the dialogue is brimming with possibilities for discovery and articulation of new depths of understanding. But the truth that gradually emerges at each stage of this process is necessarily partial. It both discloses and conceals what is given in the subject matter uttered by the tradition in the text. The under-

---

[55] Gadamer, *Truth and Method,* 358–59 (German, 340–41).
[56] Ibid., 368 (German, 350).

standing of what is there is never complete or absolute; it is limited because hermeneutical experience itself is limited. The act of understanding can never escape its own historicity.

In Gadamer's schema, all hermeneutical experience has this dialogic structure, starting from a common ground with the text of the subject matter of understanding. Once the hermeneutical subject is claimed by a text, one must respond to it. One's response is directed toward uncovering what the text means, not merely as a statement from the past but from the standpoint of one's current horizon of understanding. This is not just a subjective determination of meaning, as if the hermeneutical subject were asking what the text means to himself alone. For in order to ask what the text is saying now, one must determine the larger question that lies behind the text itself, the question to which the text is an answer, as well as the present situation in which one stands. By going behind the text in search of the question that called it into being, one can begin to understand the wider questions the text engages. In turn, one can ask questions of the text which will elicit truth that can be comprehended by everyone, not merely peripheral information of interest to a single person.[57] This is one reason why literary classics are granted so much esteem: they function by addressing the great questions of universal scope that have the potential of drawing many souls into

---

[57] Like the Hegelian dialectic, each new horizon of understanding surpasses previous horizons. But unlike Hegelian dialectic, this process does not result in an absolute knowledge that would ultimately overcome the historically conditioned experience of the interpreter himself. The dialectic is theoretically endless: "The adequate formulation of the truth is an unending venture which goes forward only in approximations and repeated attempts. The concreteness of the logical instinct in the casing of words, types of statements, and sentences themselves bear the speculative content and indeed are an integral part of the 'expression' in which spirit presents itself." See Gadamer, "Hegel and the Dialectic of the Ancient Philosophers," 33. But this theoretical endlessness is barred by the "negative" part of the dialectic, where the particular moment of understanding reaches an impasse. The subject comes up against the limits imposed by our own finite capacities for understanding. See Hans-Georg Gadamer, "Dialectic and Sophism in Plato's *Seventh Letter*," in *Dialogue and Dialectic: Eight Hermeneutical Studies on Plato*, trans. P. Christopher Smith (New Haven: Yale University Press, 1980), 103–4n.

a new common ground of solid and transforming engagement from which the truth of new understandings can emerge.

Alienation and the Fusion of Horizons

As we suggested earlier, a major problem for understanding arises when one feels estranged from one's own tradition, when one discovers that in hermeneutical experience of the world, one feels alienated from the dominant historical and cultural tradition that would claim us and would continue to speak to us. This is a particular problem in the transmission of Christian faith, for many of the dogmatic expressions of faith come from historical, cultural, or intellectual worlds quite different from the ones we know.[58] Even some contemporary church teachings, for example, the prohibition of the ordination of women, seem incomprehensible to some people and seem to have originated within contexts far removed from their own. Gadamer recognizes that this modern experience of estrangement is often the starting point for engagement with the authority of a tradition:

> For us, the understanding of the Christian tradition and the tradition of classical antiquity includes an element of historical consciousness. Even if the forces binding us to the great Greco-Christian tradition are still ever so vital, our consciousness of its alien character, of no longer belonging unquestioningly to it, determines us all.[59]

Caught within alienation, people may also find that they are bound up with the very tradition from which they may feel alienated, if only because they are addressed by it in a way that elicits a response, and hence a renewed effort to understand it. In the effort to understand dogmatic expressions, we begin to bridge the gulf between our own world of familiar meanings and the strange or alien worlds whence these statements come.

---

[58] For an earlier treatment of this problem, see Paul Crowley, "Philosophic Hermeneutics and Dogmatic Tradition, *Krisis* (Houston) 5/6 (1986–87): 48–60.

[59] Hans-Georg Gadamer, "On the Problem of Self-Understanding," in *Philosophical Hermeneutics,* trans. David E. Linge (Berkeley: University of California Press, 1976), 46.

Gadamer calls this conscious mediation by the interpreter of the history of the effects of past meanings on the current act of understanding the merging or "fusion of horizons" [*Horizontverschmeltzung*].[60] This metaphor of fusion could well serve as a model for understanding how dogma functions as classic in a pluralistic church. In a pluralistic context, many local horizons of understanding converge upon the horizon of the tradition represented by the dogmatic expression. In this fusion of horizons the horizon of the tradition is presented in and through the dogmatic expression, functioning now as a classic. As the local churches engage in dialogue with the dogmatic expression, allowing the expression to address and claim them, they in turn look for the question that lies behind the expression in asking what this means for them. They also understand themselves as standing at a particular moment in a particular place within a much wider tradition, and as part of a world church. With this awareness, and through this process of questioning, which is really a questioning of the tradition from which the dogmatic expression comes, certain features of the horizon of the tradition become sharpened while others may disappear. For example, some local theologies in Latin America have stressed the liberating praxis of Jesus, which is one key aspect but not the entire portrait of Jesus that the tradition gives us in its dogmatic expressions. The operation of the moment of application (e.g., the historical circumstances of the local church) and of prejudices (the various predispositions toward the subject matter) both partially determine what comes into view. The result of this process is the emergence of a new horizon of meaning which properly should not obliterate the horizon from which the dogmatic utterance speaks, but which nevertheless emerges as a distinct horizon of understanding intrinsically dependent on the old.

This new horizon could actually be seen to preserve the difference between past and present, and between local and universal, by allowing the tradition to be effective in the particularity of the worlds of local churches. For example, there is already evident within the Catholic Church more than one possible interpretation by some of the local churches of the tradition of priestly celibacy. Granting this kind of richness of understanding of the tradition, the horizon of the tradition could continue to appear and function

---

[60] Gadamer, *Truth and Method*, 305–7 (German, 289–90).

within the particular horizons of the local churches. While shades of difference in the interpretation of a particular dogmatic expression might emerge, a philosophic foundation for consensus could also be established.

Dogma in the most precisely defined and recent sense of the word, as an authoritatively taught proposition of faith, can play a unifying role in the life of faith if it is seen to function as a classic. Dogma as classic would not itself constrict the effort of the entire church to understand its faith anew; it could instead, like a classic, rivet the attention of the church as the horizons of the faith tradition and of current experience are brought together. Out of this newly interpreted "classic" new shades of meaning could emerge, even as the content of the dogmatic classic itself perdures. In some cases, as Rahner explained, new statements would emerge, and the tradition would continue to thrive.

Critically evaluated, Gadamer's hermeneutical model offers a philosophical matrix within which to imagine dogma functioning as an instrument of ecclesial unity. First, when approached as a classic, it speaks from the tradition with authority but is also subject to a continuing interpretation. In the fusion of horizons, the heart of the tradition remains intact even as it is reinterpreted in and through the dogmatic expression, functioning as a classic. Second, this continuing interpretation takes place from a multiplicity of perspectives, so that what is at work is not simply one horizon of the past and a contemporary horizon of the present, but several interfacing horizons, some overlapping, some converging, from a variety of angles. But they find their unity and coherence in the dogmatic expression around which they move. Third, this is a dialogic process of which the linguistic formulations of the church's experience of God's self-communication are not the starting point for approaching dogma, but are rather an intrinsic moment of that experience. The language of the dogmatic classic is not in the first instance a delimiting language, but a unifying one because it is the medium in which understanding takes place. And while the processes of understanding are inherently linguistic, the dogmatic statement is not limited in this model to a propositional entity with a life of its own beyond the context of the interpreters. It includes a range of symbolic forms of faith confession. Dogma thus understood could function as an instrument of unity.

CONCLUSION

Dogmatic Pluralism and Ecclesial Unity

In view of these reflections on the pluralistic and ambigious nature of tradition it seems to me that the Christian community, i.e., the church, requires a continuous assessment of all its manifestations and doctrinal symbols. This assessment may well lead to a thorough rethinking of all the present criteria of ecclesial authenticity and to an always renewed search for the most adequate understanding of and response to Jesus Christ's call on us to participate in God's creative and redemptive project.

Werner G. Jeanrond[1]

The purpose of these reflections has been to retrieve a sense of the unifying function of dogma. We first noted that catholic unity can be achieved either through emphasis on universal adherence to Roman teaching or through emphasis on the consensus of faith that arises in the communion of the various local churches in faith. I have chosen to emphasize the *communio* dimension of catholicity here and to ask how dogma, broadly understood not only as teaching but also as confession of faith, could serve to further that *communio*. Unity, then, rests in the appropriation of the faith tradition in specific times and places by local churches.

In these brief concluding reflections, we take a final comprehensive look at dogma's function as idea, symbol, and classic, and propose that this threefold approach can help ground dogma as a unifying agent in faith. This grounding can be secured, however, only by a final turn to the most ancient anchors of unity, the "rule

---

[1] Jeanrond, *Theological Hermeneutics*, 180.

of faith" whence dogma originated, and the criterion of faith in Jesus Christ.

DOGMA'S THREEFOLD FUNCTION

At the outset we asked three questions of dogma: how its changing forms of expression can be reconciled with the selfsame truth of faith that it is said to convey; how dogma can mediate the faith to the "mind" of the entire church constituted of local churches; and how differences in interpreting dogmatic expressions can be accounted for. We then proposed approaching dogma under the rubrics of idea, symbol, and classic. Each of these rubrics can play a role in offering a comprehensive view of dogma as an agent of unity.

Newman's notion of dogma as "idea" of revelation means that it functions to represent the truth of revelation (the sacred impression) made on the mind of the entire church. Newman emphasized the stability of dogma's function, its ability to convey that sacred impression throughout the variations of time and place in the history of the church. His theory of development, based on the analogy of the development of an idea in the mind, guaranteed the immutability of the revealed impression, even as the forms of dogmatic expression continued to grow and change.

Rahner's notion of dogma as symbol of the transcendental experience of the divine self-communication grants a similar functional stability. The self-communication of God is the selfsame communication at all times and in all places, and it is addressed as grace to structures of human subjectivity that are universally shared by all people of the church. As symbol, dogma mediates this self-communication to such an extent that the dogmatic expression itself is ontologically identified with what it mediates. At the same time, that symbol, as a human expression, is not unsurpassable. It is subject to further refinement and development, or even to replacement by other expressions.

Gadamer's understanding of the classic opens up the possibility of seeing dogma function like a classic. The classic as a monument of a tradition transmits within itself a message from that tradition which, despite new interpretations, remains rooted in the origins of the tradition itself. Although the form in which the classic is presented, or the understandings that can be given it, do vary, the core of the tradition expressed by the classic remains intact and continues to claim its addressees with a certain authority.

While dogma understood in a threefold way as idea, symbol, and classic helps address the traditional Catholic concern for guaranteeing the immutability of revealed truth amidst the changing forms of dogmatic expression, each of these rubrics gives emphasis to other concerns that bear on dogma's unifying function within a pluralistic church. Newman's notion of dogma as idea emphasizes the fact that this revelation is impressed on the many minds that constitute the one mind of the church. This leads to the possibility not only of dogmatic development but of a certain pluralism in the understanding of dogma. It is because of the reality of this pluralism, evident to him through his historical studies, that he placed such great emphasis later in his thought on the *conspiratio pastorum et fidelium* in arriving at an authoritative articulation of the faith. While paying due deference to the role of the hierarchical magisterium in arriving at ecclesial unity, he also placed great emphasis on consensus building as a foundation for that unity. This emphasis is echoed in Rahner's account of the collective search for truth, reflecting a more modern understanding of the church as a communion of many churches with their respective local traditions.

In turn, Rahner's approach to dogma as mediating symbol strongly emphasizes the fact that dogma is more than it appears: that the dogmatic expression is the form of God's address to the spiritual subjectivity of the church. Because Rahner's point of departure was transcendental experience, which emphasizes the individual subject's experience of God, his approach allowed for a radical emphasis on the fact that divine revelation is a transcendental reality, one that is communicated not only to one historical epoch or sector of the church, but at all times to all people of the church. This means that, because there will be particular local categorical mediations of revelation, dogmatic expressions at the local levels in a world church may well be pluriform. It also means, of course, as it did for Newman, that the need for a central teaching authority is indisputable. However, the unity that dogma can help provide starts not with the central teachings per se but rather with the transcendental experience of God that is offered to the entire church in both its universality and its particularity. Dogma is an instrument of unity because it is a symbol of the divine self-communication that establishes ecclesial communion.

Finally, Gadamer's hermeneutical framework, especially his notion of hermeneutical experience, places great emphasis on the need to recognize that classic forms of human expression, including dogmatic ones, must be received, interpreted, and appropriated even as they are authoritatively transmitted. Dogmatic expressions, like the classic, are subject to ongoing understanding because they are monuments of living tradition. Gadamer's metaphor of the fusion of horizons around the dogmatic classic, reached through dialogue with the classic monument, invites the imagining of an analogous convergence of the horizons of the local churches around the dogmatic classic in an ongoing process of understanding through dialogue concerning what these dogmatic classics convey.

This threefold approach to dogma begins to help secure its unifying function as an instrument toward the building of a communion of faith: through the unfolding idea that emphasizes the mind of the church converging toward a communal consensus; through the mediating symbol that conveys the self-communication of God to the spiritual subjectivity of the church; and through the interpreted classic that serves as the focal point of the ongoing intra-ecclesial dialogue about the truth of revelation. Still, if dogma is to be understood in the broader, confessional sense proposed here, then we must still search for something more: By what foundational criterion can we understand it to function as idea, symbol, or classic in such a way that the church can avoid the theological relativism and ecclesial chaos that dogma as a principle should properly defend against?

RECOVERING THE *REGULA FIDEI*

Granted the indispensability of a universal teaching office in the church, we must still ask how various understandings of dogma, from multiple perspectives, can find a common point of reference in the language of faith itself. Here we can only make a theological suggestion: a retrieval of the unifying function of the ancient *regula fidei* (the "rule of faith" or "measure of faith").

Dogma must have sufficient propositional structure in order to function as doctrine, but its nature cannot be limited to the grammar and syntax of propositions. For dogma itself, as we have seen, is intimately bound up with the church's confession of faith and emerges from it. As the early church strove for doctrinal unity, it sought to root that teaching in its confessional practices and traditions, which could serve as a measure of doctrinal authenticity. A rather flexible but minimalist measure of the content of the faith tradition emerged in the *regula fidei*, a normative but not always elaborately formulated common stock of belief and confession that eventually developed into formal teaching.

Prior to the First Council of Nicaea, it was the *regula fidei*, not formally promulgated dogma, that constituted the common core of catholic faith; no fully developed universal creeds were circulating among the faithful. In the East, and in the West, appeal was made instead to various "rules of faith" also called the "rule of truth" or the "rule of the church."[2] Some mention of the Father, Son, and Spirit in the rule of faith was reflected in a triadic structure that became the foundational structure of later trinitarian creeds. The rule was rooted in revelation, transmitted in scripture and the apostolic sacramental traditions, and in the baptismal catechesis and preaching of the churches. Its formal content, no matter how variously it was understood, was universally accepted because of its apostolic origin.[3] And it was natively doxological: It was rooted in the entire church's confession, in every quarter, of God as Father, Son, and Holy Spirit, a formula that united all Christians in the

[2] J. N. D. Kelly maintains that rules of faith in the second and early third centuries were not tied to standard formulae, and that they were not creeds. "[E]ven if some of the summaries current in the Church, especially the briefer ones, approximated to creeds, it is important to be on one's guard against applying this description to them too hastily." *Early Christian Creeds*, 3d ed. (New York: Longman, 1972), 96. The patristic scholar Joseph Lienhard concurs: "The [Arian] crisis of 318 was part of a larger movement: a movement from the rule of faith to theology, from the language of confession to the language of reflection, from belief to speculation on what was believed." "The 'Arian' Controversy: Some Categories Reconsidered," *Theological Studies* 48 (1987): 415–37, at 420.

[3] Joseph F. Mitros, "The Norm of Faith in the Patristic Age," *Theological Studies* 29 (1968): 452–53.

waters of baptism.[4] Thus, the rule of faith was transmitted to the newly baptized through the process of catechesis and in the baptismal liturgy itself, which was celebrated after a ritual dialogue between the catechumen and the church.[5]

The rule of faith therefore constituted the fundamental theological backbone for an emerging tradition of faith that came to be expressed in dogmatic classics. This emerging tradition, which initially was able to accommodate a wide variety of dogmatic expressions and local theologies, reached a point of crisis when the means could not be found to reconcile certain interpretations of scripture with these rather lean expressions of faith. In the Arian crisis, the understanding of salvation, and of Jesus' relation to the Father, rested on the interpretation of scriptural texts.[6] Indeed, Athanasius, the leading opponent of Arius, accused him of having read the scriptures too narrowly and of being out of step with the mind of the larger church.[7] The result was what could be called the first universally promulgated dogmatic statement, the Creed of Nicaea. Even after Nicaea, various local creeds continued to be used in baptismal catechesis "and became Nicene by the insertion of the par-

[4] Lienhard adds: "The rule of faith and the *lex orandi* were clear and accepted by all. For centuries Christians had believed in one God, the Father, and in His Son Jesus Christ, and in the Holy Spirit. They had prayed to God the Father through His Son Jesus Christ, their Lord. And they had baptized in the name of the Father, and of the Son, and of the Holy Spirit. . . . Disagreement came when theologians tried to express, in the language of speculation, how Christian monotheism and the doctrine of Christ's deity could be reconciled." "The 'Arian' Controversy," 420–21.

[5] See Damien van den Eynde, *Les Normes de l'enseignment chrétien dans la littérature patristique des trois premiers siècles* (Paris: Gabalda, 1933), 291.

[6] Earlier, Clement of Alexandria had insisted on the scriptural foundations of the *regula fidei*, in both the Old and New Testaments. For Irenaeus, the "rule of truth" was the criterion that would be used to distinguish true from false interpretations of scripture. Thus, a hermeneutical principle derived from scripture could itself be used as a hermeneutical principle for the interpretation of scripture itself. See Mitros, "Norm of Faith," 459; and van den Eynde, *Normes*, 291. In the Arian controversy, key biblical texts in question were Philippians 2; 2 Corinthians 2; Hebrews 1 and 3; Ps. 45:7–8; Isa. 1:2; and the famous Prov. 8:22.

[7] See Rowan Williams, *Arius: Heresy and Tradition* (London: Darton, Longman & Todd, 1987), 113.

ticular agreed formulae into each."[8] And thus a dogmatic dimension of the faith tradition began to grow, from a rather pliable *regula fidei* to a more emphatic dogmatic expression of faith that would serve as a criterion of orthodoxy and a point of controversy, leading in later centuries to an eventual abstraction of dogma as proposition from other forms of faith expression.

Rahner argued, however, that the tendency to limit creedal statements to the most ancient promulgated forms is not a requirement of faith.[9] The "Ur-classic" for the church is not the Creed of Nicaea itself but the underlying "rule of faith" out of which it emerged, and which allowed for an intra-ecclesial dialogue about the meaning of faith. While the Creed of Nicaea, the Chalcedonian Definition, and certain other monuments of the faith tradition will always serve as points of reference and as dogmatic classics, the "rule of faith" could also serve to undergird further elaborations of faith, and the emergence of new dogmatic expressions of faith.

A contemporary recovery of the *regula fidei* within the life of the church as a criterion of dogmatic unity could aid as well the recovery of dogma as a unifying factor within the faith tradition, opening up possibilities for new interpretations of some old teachings, but aligning these interpretations with the ancient *regula fidei*.

The shape of this *regula fidei*, which is something other than a fully elaborated catechism, remains to be determined. But if it were adequately articulated, it could also allow for local variations of interpretation and practice, not concerning the essentials of faith but certainly concerning those matters that tend to create tensions between local churches and Rome. This, however, leads into regions of ecclesiology that cannot preoccupy us here.

ANALOGIA CHRISTI

Still, some might argue, the contemporary church is beset with so much pluralism that an even more fundamental standard should be sought, one to which an ultimate theological, even authoritative magisterial appeal could be made in the search for unity. For example, in recent discussion over the disputed question of the ordina-

---

[8] See Frances Young, *The Making of the Creeds* (London: SCM, 1991), 3.
[9] Rahner, *Foundations of Christian Faith*, 448–54.

tion of women, it has been suggested that the final criterion should be not tradition alone but the person of Jesus Christ.[10] In other words, invocation of the person of Christ as he is presented in the scriptures, and interpreted by the church, should stand as the final criterion for unity.

Roger Haight offers some consideration of this question in his *Dynamics of Theology*.[11] Haight begins with revelation, which, following Rahner, "consists in God being ever present in personal self-communication with the history of human freedom. God is really present to and enters into real dialogue with human beings."[12] While this revelation is singularly universal in that it is the revelation of the one and only God, it is pluriform in that it takes place in human history and has had many manifestations. Further, it has both an objective, historical character and a subjective, existential character, inasmuch as human beings not only participate in the public history of revelation but also personally have some experience of the God of revelation within this history. The universal and particular dimensions of revelation, and the historical and personal, are correlated in an ongoing dialogue of faith, a dialogue between the experience of God through various media of revelation and the interpretation of this experience in the language of belief.

In one sense, then, the experience of God in revelation develops.[13] Taking Tillich's distinction between original and dependent revelation, Haight argues that dependent revelation, "the continuation of this [original] revelational experience in history in the form of a religious tradition," is subject to change:

> It is the process of God revealing and being revealed to the vital experience of ever more people who encounter God in new ways. In so doing they interpret God differently, understand God with new

[10] See, e.g., Hermann J. Pottmeyer, "Refining the Question about Women's Ordination," *America* 175 (October 26, 1996): 16–18, and the critical response to Pottmeyer's proposal by Joseph A. Fitzmyer, "Fidelity to Jesus and the Ordination of Women," *America* 175 (December 28, 1996): 9–12.

[11] Roger Haight, *Dynamics of Theology* (New York: Paulist, 1990).

[12] Ibid., 65.

[13] Ibid., 81–82.

categorical concepts, relate their experience to the world in changing historical contexts, use different languages and language systems, reinterpret the first expressions of revelation in relation to new problems and in response to new questions. Not only does the interpretation of the "object" of original Christian revelation change, but also in myriad different ways the experience itself in revelation changes in the historical course of dependent revelation.[14]

If the experience of God in revelation can be said to change, then the interpretation of this experience will reflect this change. And the language of belief expressed in dogmatic classics—creeds, doctrines, and theological propositions—which should not be confused with revelation itself, will nevertheless partly express the interpreted meaning of revelation.[15] That which would unite these varying linguistic expressions of faith would be the fundamental reality of the "experiential encounter with God mediated by Jesus . . . that God is, that God is personal, and that God is boundless love." Haight explains:

> This formula is not reductionist nor in any way exclusive of other things that may be said of God, human existence standing before this God, and the world. It is precisely non-reductionistic and inclusive: it contains by implication the whole of Christian interpretation at any given time. This then points to the basic experience to which an appeal must be made for interpreting Christian theological statements for yesterday, today, and into the future.[16]

Haight's appeal to a fundamental religious experience of God in Jesus Christ is the foundation not only for the universality of faith but also for the legitimacy of its pluriformity, and of the multiplicity of theological discourses and dogmatic expressions.

What is emerging in systematic theology, as well as in history, biblical theology, and scriptural studies, is a mapping of many experiences to create a picture of the whole.[17] These manifold experi-

---

[14] Ibid.

[15] Ibid., 84.

[16] Ibid., 85.

[17] This is attributable in part to the influence of the "new historicism," which refrains from making sweeping claims about a single experience of faith in the early Christian communities, but represents instead a range of local experiences and theologies evident in the New Testament itself, all

ences are, as Alwyd Shorter has suggested, immediate, "even when the interpretation of that experience and the language in which the interpretation is expressed are influenced by a collective cultural tradition."[18] He argues that the faith statements of local communities of faith and regional churches find their coherence in the Christ event, and their meaning to the degree that they are interpretations and applications of what these communities believe "about the presence of the risen Christ among them, about their relationship to him and to one another in him."[19] Needless to say, such a suggestion is laden with the potential pitfalls. The meaning of Jesus Christ as central and fundamental criterion is itself a hermeneutical challenge that involves not only the weight of the transmitted dogmatic tradition in teaching and confession of faith, but also the current historical engagement with that tradition in the community of the church.[20]

Nevertheless, the person of Jesus Christ, not only as historical figure but as abiding mystery, is the final appeal to which the contemporary church must return, not through apodictic claims of special knowledge of the will of Christ but through the church's ongoing participation in the life of the risen Christ. This may well require a creative and critical retrieval of a sense of the church as the organic Body of Christ. If the Christ of the faith tradition, functioning as a *regula fidei*, expressed through scripture and the dogmatic classics of that tradition and articulated in local faith expressions, is the prime analogue of all dogmatic expressions of faith, there will be room for a pluralism of experience and of faith expression. Of more fundamental importance, there will be room for hope that the church is in fact moving into God's open future.

---

united in the common analogue of the risen Jesus. See John R. Donahue, "The Changing Shape of New Testament Theology," *Theological Studies* 50 (1989): 314–35.

[18] Shorter, *Revelation and Its Interpretation*, 11.
[19] Ibid., 151.
[20] See Jeanrond, *Theological Hermeneutics*, 180.

Works Cited

Alberigo, Giuseppe, et al., eds. *The Reception of Vatican II*. Washington, D.C.: Catholic University of America, 1987.

Alszeghy, Zoltán. "The '*Sensus Fidei*' and the Development of Dogma." In *Vatican II: Assessment and Perspectives*, vol. 1. Ed. René Latourelle. New York: Paulist, 1988.

Bardy, G. "Vincent of Lérins." In *Dictionnaire de théologie catholique*, vol. 15. Paris: Letouzey, 1923–72.

Bévenot, Maurice. "*Traditiones* in the Council of Trent." *Heythrop Journal* 4 (1963): 333–47.

Bonino, J. Miguez. "The Reception of Vatican II in Latin America." *Ecumenical Review* 37 (1985): 266–74.

Bossuet, J. B. *Histoire des variations des Eglises protestantes*. Vol. 14, *Oeuvres complètes de Bossuet*. Ed. F. Lachat. Paris: Louis Vivès, 1883.

Branick, Vincent. *An Ontology of Understanding: Karl Rahner's Metaphysics of Knowledge in the Context of Modern German Hermeneutics*. Diss., Fribourg, 1971. St. Louis: Marianist, 1971.

Brekelmans, Antonius. "Professions de Foi dans l'église primitive: origine et fonction." *Concilium* 51 (1970): 39.

Brown, Raymond E. *Biblical Exegesis and Church Doctrine*. New York: Paulist, 1985.

Chadwick, Owen. *From Bossuet to Newman: The Idea of Doctrinal Development*. Cambridge: Cambridge University Press, 1957.

Chrismann, Philipp Neri. *Regula fidei Catholicae et collectio dogmatum credendorum*. Wirceburgi: Stahelianis, 1854.

Congar, Yves M.-J. *Diversity and Communion*. Trans. John Bowden. Mystic, Conn.: Twenty-Third, 1985.

——. *La Tradition et les traditions*. Vol. 1, *Essai historique*. Paris: Arthème Fayard, 1960; Vol. 2, *Essai théologique*. Paris: Librarie Arthème Fayard, 1963. Eng. trans. *Tradition and Traditions: An Historical and a*

Theological Essay. Trans. Michael Nasey and Thomas Rainborough. New York: Macmillan, 1966.

Congregation for the Doctrine of the Faith. "Instruction on Certain Aspects of the 'Theology of Liberation.'" *Origins* 14/13 (September 13, 1984): 193–204.

———. "Instruction on Christian Freedom and Liberation." *Origins* 15/44 (April 17, 1986): 713–28.

———. "Reply to the *dubium* concerning the Teaching Contained in the Apostolic Letter *Ordinatio Sacerdotalis.*" *Origins* 25/24 (November 30, 1995): 401–5.

Crowley, Paul G. "Catholicity, Inculturation and Newman's *Sensus Fidelium.*" *Heythrop Journal* 33 (1992): 161–74.

———. "Philosophic Hermeneutics and Dogmatic Tradition." *Krisis* (Houston) 5/6 (1986–87): 48–60.

Davey, R. Nicholas. "A Response to P. Christopher Smith." In *Continental Philosophy IV: Gadamer and Hermeneutics.* Ed. Hugh J. Silverman. New York: Routledge, 1991.

Dhanis, E. "Révélation explicite et implicite." *Gregorianum* 34 (1953): 187–237.

Denziger, Heinrich. *Enchiridion Symbolorum Definitionum et Declarationum de Rebus Fidei et Morum.* 38th ed. Ed. Peter Hünermann. Freiburg: Herder, 1991.

Donahue, John R. "The Changing Shape of New Testament Theology." *Theological Studies* 50 (1989): 314–35.

Dublancy, E. "Dogme." In *Dictionnaire de théologie catholique,* vol. 4. Paris: Letouzey, 1923–72.

Dulles, Avery. *The Catholicity of the Church.* Oxford: Clarendon, 1985.

———. *The Survival of Dogma: Faith, Authority, and Dogma in a Changing World.* Garden City, N.Y.: Doubleday, 1973. Reprint, New York: Crossroad, 1985.

Dunn, James D. G. *Unity and Diversity in the New Testament: An Inquiry into the Character of Earliest Christianity.* 2d ed. London: SCM, 1990.

Dupré, Louis. *Passage to Modernity: An Essay in the Hermeneutics of Nature and Culture.* New Haven: Yale University Press, 1993.

Dych, William V. "Theology in a New Key." In *A World of Grace: An Introduction to the Themes and Foundations of Karl Rahner's Theology.* Ed. Leo O'Donovan. New York: Seabury, 1980.

Elert, Werner. *Die Kirche und ihre Dogmengeschichte.* Munich: Evangelischer Presseverband, 1950.

Elze, M. "Der Begriff des Dogmas in der Alten Kirche." *Zeitschrift für Theologie und Kirche* 61 (1964): 421–38.

Eno, Robert B. "Consensus and Doctrine: Three Ancient Views." *Eglise et Théologie* 9 (1978): 473–83.

———. *The Rise of the Papacy.* Wilmington, Del.: Michael Glazier, 1990.

Femiano, Samuel D. *Infallibility of the Laity: The Legacy of Newman.* New York: Herder & Herder, 1967.

Fitzmyer, Joseph A. "Fidelity to Jesus and the Ordination of Women." *America* 175 (December 28, 1996): 9–12.

Fitzpatrick, Joseph P. *One Church, Many Cultures: The Challenge of Diversity.* Kansas City, Mo.: Sheed & Ward, 1987.

Foucault, Michel. *The Archeology of Knowledge.* New York: Pantheon, 1972.

Fransen, Piet. "Unity and Confessional Statements: Historical and Theological Inquiry of Roman Catholic Traditional Conceptions." *Bijdragen* 33 (1972): 2–38.

Fries, Heinrich. *Fundamental Theology.* Trans. Robert J. Daly. Washington, D.C.: Catholic University of America, 1996.

Gadamer, Hans-Georg. "Dialectic and Sophism in Plato's *Seventh Letter.*" In *Dialogue and Dialectic: Eight Hermeneutical Studies on Plato.* Trans. P. Christopher Smith. New Haven: Yale University Press, 1980.

———. "Hegel and the Dialectic of the Ancient Philosophers." *Hegel's Dialectic.* Trans. P. Christopher Smith. New Haven: Yale University Press, 1976.

———. "On the Problem of Self-Understanding." In *Philosophical Hermeneutics.* Trans. David E. Linge. Berkeley: University of California Press, 1976.

———. "On the Universality of the Hermeneutical Problem." In *Philosophical Hermeneutics.* Trans. David E. Linge. Berkeley: University of California Press, 1976.

———. *Truth and Method.* 2d. rev. ed. Trans. Joel Weinsheimer and Donald G. Marshall. New York: Crossroad, 1989. Originally published as *Wahrheit und Methode: Grundzüge einer philosophischen Hermeneutik.* 4. Auflage. Tübingen: J. C. B. Mohr, 1976.

Geertz, Clifford. *The Interpretation of Cultures: Selected Essays.* New York: Basic Books, 1973.

Guarino, Thomas J. "Vincent of Lerins and the Hermeneutical Question." *Gregorianum* 75 (1994): 491–523.

Habermas, Jürgen. *Knowledge and Human Interests.* Trans. Jeremy J. Shapiro. Boston: Beacon, 1971.

Haight, Roger. *An Alternate Vision: An Interpretation of Liberation Theology.* New York: Paulist, 1985.

———. "The Case for Spirit Christology." *Theological Studies* 53 (1992): 257–87.

———. *Dynamics of Theology.* New York: Paulist, 1990.

Himes, Michael. "The Ecclesiological Significance of Reception of Doctrine." *Heythrop Journal* 33 (1992): 146–60.

Heidegger, Martin. *Being and Time.* Trans. John Macquarrie and Edward Robinson. New York: Harper & Row, 1962.

——. "On the Essence of Truth." In *Existence and Being*. Trans. R. F. C. Hull and Alan Crick. Chicago: Henry Regnery, 1949.

Hoy, David Couzens. *The Critical Circle: Literature, History and Philosophical Hermeneutics*. Berkeley: University of California Press, 1982.

Hume, David. *Treatise of Human Nature*. Ed. Ernest C. Mossner. Baltimore: Pelican, 1969.

International Theological Commission. "On the Interpretation of Dogmas." *Origins* 20/1 (May 17, 1990): 1–14.

——. *El Pluralismo teológico*. Madrid: Biblioteca de Autores Cristianos, 1976.

Jeanrond, Werner G. *Text and Interpretation as Categories of Theological Thinking*. Trans. Thomas J. Wilson. New York: Crossroad, 1988.

——. *Theological Hermeneutics: Development and Significance*. New York: Crossroad, 1991.

Jedin, Hubert. *A History of the Council of Trent*. Trans. E. Graf. St. Louis: Herder & Herder, 1961.

John Paul II, Pope. *Ut Unum Sint*. *Origins* 25/4 (June 8, 1995): 35–38.

Kasper, Walter. *Dogma unter dem Wort Gottes*. Mainz: Matthias-Grünewald, 1965.

Keble, John. *Keble's Assize Sermon*. London: Mowbray, 1931.

Kelly, J. N. D. *Early Christian Creeds*. 3d ed. New York: Longman, 1972.

Kilmartin, Edward. "The Catholic Tradition of Eucharistic Theology: Towards the Third Millennium." *Theological Studies* 55 (1994): 405–57.

Kittel, Rudolf. "dógma." In *Theological Dictionary of the New Testament*, vol. 2. Trans. Geoffrey W. Bromiley. Grand Rapids, Mich.: Eerdmans, 1964.

Komonchak, Joseph A. "The Church Universal as the Communion of Local Churches." In *Where Does the Church Stand?* Ed. Giuseppe Alberigo and Gustavo Gutierrez. New York: Seabury, 1981.

——. "The Local Realization of the Church." In *The Reception of Vatican II*. Ed. Giuseppe Alberigo, et al. Washington, D.C.: Catholic University of America, 1987.

Krieger, David J. *The New Universalism: Foundations for a Global Theology*. Maryknoll, N.Y.: Orbis, 1991.

Lash, Nicholas. *Change in Focus: A Study of Doctrinal Change and Continuity*. London: Sheed & Ward, 1973.

——. *Easter in Ordinary: Reflections on Human Experience and the Knowledge of God*. Charlottesville: University Press of Virginia, 1988.

——. *Newman on Development: The Search for an Explanation in History*. Shepherdstown, W.V.: Patmos, 1973.

——. "The Notions of 'Implicit' and 'Explicit' Reason in Newman's University Sermons: A Difficulty." *Heythrop Journal* 11 (1970): 48–54.

Lienhard, Joseph. "The 'Arian' Controversy: Some Categories Reconsidered." *Theological Studies* 48 (1987): 415–37.

Lindbeck, George A. *The Nature of Doctrine: Religion and Theology in a Post-Liberal Age.* Philadelphia: Westminster, 1984.

Lindgens, Godehard. "Pluralismus und Christentum: Studie zur katholischen Theorie über das Verhältnis von Pluralismus und Wahrheit." *Freiburger Zeitschrift für Philosophie und Theologie* 29 (1982): 465–87.

Linge, David. "Editor's Introduction." In *Philosophical Hermeneutics.* Berkeley: University of California Press, 1976.

MacIntyre, Alasdair. *After Virtue.* 2d ed. Notre Dame, Ind.: University of Notre Dame Press, 1984.

Mahoney, John. *The Making of Moral Theology: A Study of the Roman Catholic Tradition.* Oxford: Clarendon, 1987.

Marín-Sola, Francisco. *La Evolución homogénea del dogma católico.* 3d ed. Madrid: Biblioteca de Autores Cristianos, 1952.

McBrien, Richard. "The Ecclesiology of the Local Church." *Thought* 66 (1991): 359–67.

McGovern, Arthur F. *Liberation Theology and Its Critics: Towards an Assessment.* Maryknoll, N.Y.: Orbis, 1989.

Meier, John. *Antioch and Rome: New Testament Cradles of Catholic Christianity.* New York: Paulist, 1983.

Mitchell, W. J. T. "Pluralism as Dogmatism." *Critical Inquiry* 12 (Spring 1986): 494–502.

Mitros, Joseph F. "The Norm of Faith in the Patristic Age." *Theological Studies* 29 (1968): 452–53.

Newman, John Henry. *The Arians of the Fourth Century.* 5th ed. London: Pickering, 1983.

———. *Apologia pro vita sua.* Ed. David J. DeLaura. New York: Norton, 1968.

———. *Certain Difficulties Felt by Anglicans in Catholic Teaching.* 2 vols. London: Longmans, 1888.

———. *An Essay on the Development of Christian Doctrine.* 1878 rev. ed. Ed. Charles Frederick Harrold. London: Longmans, 1949.

———. *Lectures on the Prophetical Office of the Church, Viewed Relatively to Romanism and Popular Protestantism.* London: Rivington, 1837.

———. *Newman's University Sermons: Fifteen Sermons Preached before the University of Oxford 1826–43 by John Henry Newman.* Reprint of 1871 (3d) ed. London: S.P.C.K., 1970.

———. *On Consulting the Faithful in Matters of Doctrine.* Ed. John Coulson. London: Geoffrey Chapman, 1961.

———. "Tract 90. Remarks on Certain Passages in the Thirty-nine Articles." *Tracts for the Times,* vol. 6. Oxford: J. Vincent, 1842.

Noonan, John T. "Development in Moral Doctrine." *Theological Studies* 54 (1993): 662–77.

O'Collins, Gerald. *The Case Against Dogma.* New York: Paulist, 1975.

O'Connell, Marvin R. *Critics on Trial: An Introduction to the Catholic Modernist Crisis.* Washington, D.C.: Catholic University of America, 1994.

O'Donovan, Leo. "Orthopraxis and Theological Method in Karl Rahner." *Proceedings of the Catholic Theological Society of America* 35 (1980): 48–51.

Ommen, Thomas B. *The Hermeneutic of Dogma.* Diss., Missoula, Mont.: Scholars Press, 1975.

———. "The Hermeneutic of Dogma." *Theological Studies* 35 (1974): 605–31.

Owen, H. P. "Dogma." In *Encyclopedia of Philosophy,* vol. 2. New York: Macmillan, 1967.

Palmer, Richard. *Hermeneutics: Interpretation Theory in Schleiermacher, Dilthey, Heidegger, and Gadamer.* Evanston, Ill: Northwestern, 1969.

Pannenberg, Wolfhart. "Hermeneutic and Universal History." *Basic Questions in Theology,* vol. 1. Trans. George Kehm. Philadelphia: Fortress, 1970.

Pelikan, Jaroslav. *Development of Christian Doctrine: Some Historical Prolegomena.* New Haven: Yale, 1969.

———. *The Emergence of the Catholic Tradition.* Vol. 1 of *The Christian Tradition: A History of the Development of Doctrine.* Chicago: University of Chicago Press, 1971.

———. *Historical Theology: Continuity and Change in Christian Doctrine.* London: Hutchinson, 1971.

———. *The Spirit of Eastern Christendom.* Vol. 2 of *The Christian Tradition: A History of the Development of Doctrine.* Chicago: University of Chicago Press, 1974.

Pohier, Jacques, ed. *Christian Ethics: Uniformity, Universality, Pluralism.* New York: Seabury, 1981.

Pontifical Biblical Commission. "The Interpretation of the Bible in the Church." *Origins* 23/29 (January 6, 1994): 497–524.

Pottmeyer, Hermann J. "Refining the Question about Women's Ordination." *America* 175 (October 26, 1996): 16–18.

Principe, Walter. "Catholicity, Inculturation and Liberation Theology: Do They Mix?" *Franciscan Studies* 47 (1987): 24–43.

———. "Catholicity: Threat or Help to Identity?" *Identity Issues and World Religions.* Bedford Park, Australia: Australian Association for the Study of Religions, 1986.

———. "The Hermeneutic of Roman Catholic Dogmatic Statements." *Sciences Religieuses* 2 (1972): 157–75.

———. "When 'Authentic' Teachings Change." *The Ecumenist* 25/26 (1987): 70–73.

Quinn, John R. "Cardinal Newman: A Study in Integrity." *Origins* 20/35 (February 7, 1991): 579–84.

Rahner, Karl. "Basic Theological Interpretation of the Second Vatican Council." In *Theological Investigations,* vol. 20. Trans. Edward Quinn. New York: Crossroad, 1986.

———. "Considerations on the Development of Dogma." In *Theological Investigations,* vol. 4. Trans. Kevin Smyth. Baltimore: Helicon, 1966. Originally published as "Überlegungen zur Dogmenentwicklung." In *Schriften zur Theologie,* Band 4. Zurich: Benziger, 1961.

———. "Current Problems in Christology." In *Theological Investigations,* vol. 1. Trans. Cornelius Ernst. London: Darton, Longman & Todd, 1961.

———. "The Development of Dogma." In *Theological Investigations,* vol. 1. Trans. Cornelius Ernst. Baltimore: Helicon, 1961. Originally published as "Zur Frage der Dogmenentwicklung." In *Schriften zur Theologie,* Band 1. Zurich: Benziger, 1962.

———. *Foundations of Christian Faith: An Introduction to the Idea of Christianity.* Trans. William V. Dych. New York: Seabury, 1978.

———. *Hearers of the Word.* Trans. Michael Richards. New York: Herder & Herder, 1969. Originally published as *Hörer des Wortes: Zur Grundlegung einer Religionsphilosophie.* Ed. J. E. Metz. Munich: Kösel, 1964.

———. "On Heresy." In *Inquiries.* Trans. W. J. O'Hara. New York: Herder & Herder, 1964.

———. "Revelation." In *Sacramentum Mundi,* vol. 5. Ed. Karl Rahner and Adolf Darlap. New York: Herder & Herder, 1970.

———. "A Small Fragment 'On the Collective Finding of Truth.'" In *Theological Investigations,* vol. 6. Trans. Karl-H. and Boniface Kruger. New York: Seabury, 1974. Originally published as "Kleines Fragment 'Über die kollektive Findung der Wahrheit.'" In *Schriften zur Theologie,* Band 6. Zurich: Benziger, 1968.

———. "Scripture and Tradition." In *Theological Investigations,* vol. 6. Trans. Karl-H. and Boniface Kruger. New York: Seabury, 1974.

———. *Spirit in the World.* Trans. William V. Dych. New York: Herder & Herder, 1968. Originally published as *Geist in Welt: Zur Metaphysik der endlichen Erkenntnis bei Thomas von Aquin.* 3. Auflage. Munich: Kösel, 1964.

———. "The Teaching Office of the Church in the Present-Day Crisis of Authority." In *Theological Investigations,* vol. 12. New York: Seabury, 1974. Originally published as "Das kirchliche Lehramt in der heutigen Autoritätekrise." In *Schriften zur Theologie,* Band 9. Zurich: Benziger, 1970.

———. "Theology in the New Testament." In *Theological Investigations,* vol. 5. Trans. Karl-H. Kruger. Baltimore: Helicon, 1966.

———. "The Theology of Symbol." In *Theological Investigations,* vol. 4. Trans. Kevin Smyth. Baltimore: Helicon, 1966. Originally published as "Zur Theologie des Symbols." In *Schriften zur Theologie,* Band 4. Zurich: Benziger, 1961.

———. "Unity of the Church—Unity of Mankind." In *Theological Investigations,* vol. 20. Trans. Edward Quinn. New York: Crossroad, 1981.

———. "What Is a Dogmatic Statement?" In *Theological Investigations,* vol 5. Trans. Karl-H. Kruger. Baltimore: Helicon, 1966. Originally published as "Was ist eine dogmatische Aussage?" In *Schriften zur Theologie,* Band 5. Zurich: Benziger, 1962.

Reiser, William. "An Essay on the Development of Dogma in a Heideggerian Context: A Non-Theological Explanation of Theological Heresy." *The Thomist* 30 (1975): 471–95.

Richard, Robert L. "Rahner's Theory of Doctrinal Development." *Proceedings of the Catholic Theological Society of America* 18 (1963): 157–89.

Schillebeeckx, Edward. *Christ: The Experience of Jesus as Lord.* New York: Crossroad, 1989.

———. *Revelation and Theology,* vol. 1. Trans. N. D. Smith. New York: Sheed & Ward, 1967.

Schneiders, Sandra M. *The Revelatory Text: Interpreting the New Testament as Sacred Scripture.* San Francisco: HarperSanFrancisco, 1991.

Schoof, T. M. *A Survey of Catholic Theology: 1800–1970.* Trans. N. D. Smith. New York: Paulist, 1970.

Schoonenberg, Piet. "Historicity and the Interpretation of Dogma." *Theology Digest* 18 (1970): 132–43.

Schreiter, Robert. *Constructing Local Theologies.* Maryknoll, N.Y.: Orbis, 1986.

Segundo, Juan Luis. *The Liberation of Dogma: Faith, Revelation and Dogmatic Teaching Authority.* Trans. Phillip Berryman. Maryknoll, N.Y.: Orbis, 1992.

Shorter, Alwyd. *Revelation and Its Interpretation.* London: Geoffrey Chapman, 1983.

Southern, R. W. *Western Society and the Church in the Middle Ages.* Vol. 2 of *The Pelican History of the Church.* Baltimore: Penguin, 1970.

Sullivan, Francis A. *Creative Fidelity: Weighing and Interpreting Documents of the Magisterium.* New York: Paulist, 1996.

———. *Magisterium: Teaching Authority in the Catholic Church.* New York: Paulist, 1983.

Tanner, Norman, ed. *Decrees of the Ecumenical Councils.* 2 vols. New York: Sheed & Ward and Georgetown, 1990.

Thomas Aquinas. *Summa theologica.* Paris: Andreae Blot, 1932.

Thomas, Owen C. "On Stepping Twice into the Same Church: Essence, Development and Pluralism." *Anglican Theological Review* 70 (1988): 293–306.

Tillard, J. M. R. *The Bishop of Rome.* Trans. John de Satgé. Wilmington, Del.: Michael Glazier, 1983.

Toulmin, Stephen. *Cosmopolis: The Hidden Agenda of Modernity.* Chicago: University of Chicago Press, 1990.

Tracy, David. *The Analogical Imagination: Christian Theology and the Culture of Pluralism.* New York: Crossroad, 1981.

van den Eynde, Damien. *Les Normes de l'enseignment chrétien dans la littéra-ture patristique des trois premiers siècles.* Paris: Gabalda, 1933.

Vincent of Lerins. "The Commonitories." *The Fathers of the Church.* Trans. Rudolph E. Morris. New York: Fathers of the Church, 1949. Cf. J.-P. Migne, ed., *Patrologiae cursus completus: Series Latina,* vol. 50. Paris, 1846.

Vorgrimler, Herbert, ed. *Commentary on the Documents of Vatican II.* 5 vols. New York: Crossroad, 1989.

——. "From *Sensus Fidei* to *Consensus Fidelium.*" In *The Authority of the Believers.* Ed. Johannes-Baptist Metz and Edward Schillebeeckx. Edinburgh: T. & T. Clark, 1985.

Walgrave, J.-H. *Newman: Le développement du dogme.* Tournai: Casterman, 1956.

Ward, Wilfrid. *The Life of John Henry Cardinal Newman.* 2 vols. New York: Longmans, 1912.

Weigel, Gustave. "Foreword." *An Essay on the Development of Christian Doctrine.* Garden City, N.Y.: Doubleday, 1960.

Weinsheimer, Joel C. *Gadamer's Hermeneutics; A Reading of Truth and Method.* New Haven: Yale, 1985.

Williams, Rowan. *Arius: Heresy and Tradition.* London: Darton, Longman & Todd, 1987.

Wright, John H. "Roger Haight's Spirit Christology." *Theological Studies* 53 (1992): 729–35.

Young, Frances. *The Making of the Creeds.* London: SCM, 1991.

Index